ENGLISH IN CONTEXT

Reading Comprehension
for Science and Technology

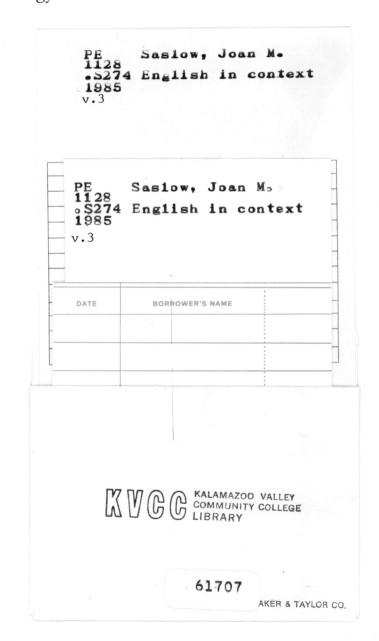

BOOK 3

ENGLISH IN CONTEXT

Reading Comprehension
for Science and Technology

Joan M. Saslow

John F. Mongillo

Prentice-Hall, Englewood Cliffs, New Jersey 07632

61707

Library of Congress Cataloging in Publication Data
(Revised for vol. 3)

APR 1 1 1985

Saslow, Joan M. (date)
   English in context.

   1. English language—Text-books for foreign
speakers.   2. English language—Technical English.
3. College readers.   4. Readers—Science.
5. Readers—Technology.   I. Mongillo, John F.
II. Title.
[PE1128.S274 1985]   428.6'4'0245   84-4800
ISBNO0-13-280025-X (pbk.: v. 1)

Editorial/production supervision and
      interior design: Barbara Alexander
Cover design: Whitman Studio, Inc.
Photo research: Teri Stratford
Manufacturing buyer: Harry P. Baisley

Cover photo credit: Courtesy NASA
Lesson opening photo credits:

1: WCO Creative Services Group; 2: Teri Leigh Stratford; 3: Carolina Biological
Supply; 4: Teri Leigh Stratford; 5: AP/Wide World Photos; 6: Teri Leigh Stratford;
7: Carl Frank, Photo Researchers, Inc.; 8: Teri Leigh Stratford; 9: Manfred Kage,
Peter Arnold, Inc.; 10: Teri Leigh Stratford

© 1986 by Prentice-Hall
A Division of Simon & Schuster, Inc.
Englewood Cliffs, New Jersey 07632

Printed in the United States of America

10 9 8 7 6 5 4 3 2 1

ISBN 0-13-280041-1   01

PRENTICE-HALL INTERNATIONAL, INC., *London*
PRENTICE-HALL OF AUSTRALIA, PTY. LIMITED, *Sydney*
EDITORA PRENTICE-HALL DO BRASIL, LTDA., *Rio de Janeiro*
PRENTICE-HALL OF CANADA, LTD., *Toronto*
PRENTICE-HALL OF INDIA PRIVATE LIMITED, *New Delhi*
PRENTICE-HALL OF JAPAN, INC., *Tokyo*
PRENTICE-HALL OF SOUTHEAST ASIA PTE. LTD., *Singapore*
WHITEHALL BOOKS LIMITED, *Wellington, New Zealand*

Contents

Preface

Purpose

English in Context: Reading Comprehension for Science and Technology is an intermediate-level reading comprehension text series for students who want concentrated practice in reading scientific and technical English. The sole purpose of this three-level text series is to build the comprehension skill. Although it is unarguably true that listening, speaking, and writing practice enhance the reading skill, practice in reading itself is a more direct route to this goal. Thus, *English in Context: Reading Comprehension for Science and Technology* elicits no production of written or spoken English, and includes no listening comprehension activities. Students at the intermediate level may already have been exposed to years of classroom practice of the "four skills." What is provided here, then, is an alternate path focused entirely on reading.

Student Profile

English in Context: Reading Comprehension for Science and Technology is intended for students who have had beginning-level courses in English, either at the secondary-school level or at the university, the technical school, or the binational institute. These students typically have had two- to three-hundred hours of classroom instruction, often in large classes. They have been exposed, at one time or another (and with greater or lesser amounts of success), to the "basic structures" of the language, and they have a fair vocabulary covering everyday activities, work, school, play, and hobbies. They function conversationally at a low level and make many mistakes in grammar, lexicon, and pronunciation. They understand more difficult language than that which they can produce on their own. Their reading ability generally corresponds to what they can say, because they have studied from texts that "strictly control" the reading narratives. These students approach all unfamiliar readings with a bilingual dictionary close at hand, since they are unskilled in deriving meaning from passages containing new words without translating every new word into their own language. They are particularly handicapped when facing a scientific or technical reading because their training has been in "everyday" English. It should be kept in mind that the students for whom these three texts in the *English in Context* series were created are not English majors, but rather are specialists (or specialists in training) in some area of science and technology.

Scope of the Series and Focus of Book Three

English in Context: Reading Comprehension for Science and Technology, Books 1 and 2 are similar in design and format, while Book 3 differs significantly. The purpose of the series as a whole is to prepare students to read authentic published source materials in any area of science or technology. The first two books presented reading selections especially written to ready students for this goal by illustrating the use of high-frequency science vocabulary and important concepts in grammar and syntax. Book 3, on the other hand, has been designed to bridge the gap between the "engineered" reading selections of Books 1 and 2 and free reading, in that it centers on REAL, UNEDITED EXCERPTS from published university-level science textbooks while maintaining a good deal of supporting exercise and explanatory material.

In addition to the lessons devoted to reading the narratives taken from published materials, Book 3 additionally devotes fully half of its content to providing practice in the use of text materials. These sections concentrate on two important areas. The first area is the use of the physical features of textbooks, such as tables of contents, appendixes, glossaries, indexes, bibliographies, and reference lists. The second part of the materials section is devoted to reading and interpreting the visual features of textbooks: charts, tables, diagrams, graphs, line drawings, and schematic illustrations.

Odd-numbered lessons are "Narrative" lessons and even-numbered lessons are "Materials" lessons. Both types are fully described below.

Working Assumptions

Underlying the development of these materials are several assumptions. The first is that scientific and technical English are English. The characteristic features of this type of writing are all found in all other forms of English. Colin R. Elliot has remarked that [except for technical terms and some more complex structures] there is little to distinguish it from any other form of writing which seeks to explain and exemplify general theories or describe processes" (ELT Journal, October 1976). J. D. Corbluth (ELT Journal, July 1975) even disagrees that there is such a thing as scientific English at all. Although other possible grammatical frameworks exist (notably Ewer's Microacts, for example), we have chosen to base these materials on the assumption that the similarities between scientific/technical English and ordinary English are greater than the differences between them, always recognizing, however, that students predictably will have difficulty with certain syntactical and grammatical features which occur frequently. Some well-recognized examples of these are passive voice, noun compounds, *if*-clauses, long preposed modifying clusters, and reduced adjective clauses. These have been given particular emphasis throughout the series.

In addition to the choice of the syntactical and grammatical features in each of the odd-numbered (Narrative) lessons, certain words were chosen for inclusion in the vocabulary sections at the beginning of these lessons. It was our working assumption that most of these words are probably not known by the student who has had the two- to three-hundred hours of English described above. These words are found over and over in scientific and technical prose. Most of them are of a type we call "subtechnical," that is, they are not highly specialized for one narrow field of interest but rather are found in writings in all areas of science and technology. It is our belief that knowing these words will greatly increase comprehension of scientific and technical narrative. Some examples of "subtechnical" words from Book 3 are *fracture, pore, correlate, shock, fuse,* and *scatter*—words that conceivably could be found in the areas of medicine, seismology, mathematics, physics, agriculture, botany, or many other fields. Another category of words or expressions (equally important to the comprehension of science narrative) is of a type less "scientific" in nature. Some examples of this type of vocabulary taken from Book 3 are *countless, conspicuous, apparently, fortuitous, to elaborate, readily,* and *yet to be determined.*

Organization and Lesson Format

NARRATIVE LESSONS (All odd-numbered lessons)

Each narrative lesson in *English in Context: Reading Comprehension for Science and Technology*, Book 3 is built around a reading selection taken from a current, well-known textbook. *All other sections of the lesson are tightly connected to the reading, either as a preparation for it or an extension of it.* In this way, *every* word and *every* exercise deals with comprehension of the central reading selection of the lesson. The following is a description of the subsections of these odd-numbered lessons.

Reading Selection

The reading selections forming the core of the odd-numbered lessons are taken from authentic published college-level textbooks. These selections have not been edited or simplified in any way. They are from two to four pages in length and cover a variety of topics: the retina, root pressure and guttation, widespread effects of air pollution, immune responses, and earthquake forecasting and control. These were chosen both because of their universal appeal and because they invariably illustrate through context vocabulary that is of use to readers. In addition to their value in vocabulary development, they are written in styles characteristic of textbook narrative as a whole and will therefore be of use in preparing students to read in their various fields of specialization. Throughout, care has been taken in ensuring THAT THE INSTRUCTOR WITH A HUMANITIES RATHER THAT A SCIENCE BACKGROUND WILL BE COMFORTABLE TEACHING THESE SELECTIONS.

All vocabulary taught in the lesson comes from that lesson's reading selection. Similarly, all comprehension exercises are based on the reading selection. A description of these features follows.

Vocabulary

The vocabulary section immediately follows the reading. All words on the list come from that lesson's reading. Each word is defined simply and directly. It is then used in the same sentence in which it appeared in the reading. When necessary or possible, an illustration is included as a further conveyor of meaning. The illustration, it should be noted, illustrates the word in its most general, universal sense. In other words, the illustration pertains to the definition, not to the specific sentence taken from the reading. This was done to ensure that students will be able to understand these words when they encounter them in their own readings. For example, in Lesson 3 the word *bundle* is defined as a "group of objects held together." The illustration is of a bundle of clothes held together with a belt. The sentence taken from the reading is "Because water-conducting xylem elements of a vascular bundle terminate in a hydathode, xylem sap is forced to flow through the hydathode." The illustration was provided to give students a visual image of what a bundle is, so that when they encounter this word in another context, they won't be mentally tied to the limited and specific use of the word in the phrase "vascular bundle."

Vocabulary Exercises

If learners remembered words after seeing them only once, then these exercises would not be necessary. It is every language teacher's experience that in order to make vocabulary "active," rigorous practice is necessary. All too often at the intermediate level, students' vocabularies stop growing because it is assumed that practice is only appropriate for beginners. A series of exercises in each of these lessons provides students with yet another opportunity to see each of the vocabulary words from that lesson in a relevant contextual sentence. These exercises are not a test. They are meant to help commit meaning to memory. Not only will each word be elicited as an answer to a question, but it also will be used several other times in items eliciting other vocabulary words as answers.

Comprehension

The remainder of each odd-numbered lesson is made up of comprehension exercises based on the reading. This section is broken into the following four subsections:

I. Meaning

Exercises in this subsection give practice in the major reading comprehension skills of:

> factual recall
> finding the main idea
> understanding new vocabulary from context
> confirmation of content

determining cause and effect
distinguishing fact from opinion
drawing conclusions

All material used in the exercise(s) is taken from the reading.

II. Reference

Exercises in the reference subsection provide practice in identifying the antecedents of words that might be ambiguous to a nonnative reader of English. Such difficult references abound in scientific prose. Some sentences provide all that is needed for the reader to identify the reference:

example: *Choose a or b to indicate the reference for the italicized word or phrase.*

The effective focal length of the relaxed eye is about 17 mm, which means that the retinal image is the same size as *that* which would be formed by a single 17 mm focal length lens. (¶ 1)
  a. the retinal image
  b. the 17 mm focal length lens

Other references have to be determined from the surrounding material and require a more in-depth comprehension of the selection as a whole.

example: *Choose a or b to indicate the reference for the italicized word or phrase.*

This is illustrated by sulfur dioxides leading to the formation of acid rain and the widespread effect of air pollution on plants. (¶ 1)
  a. formation of acid rain
  b. spreading of harmful effects more widely

III. Syntax

These subsections concentrate on comprehension of some structures and syntax patterns that are very likely to interfere with comprehension. These are: preposed modifying clusters, passive voice, *-ing* words (gerunds, participles, progressives), and adjective clauses and phrases. All exercise items here (as throughout the comprehension subsections) come from the reading selection. The following example comes from an exercise on adjective clauses and phrases.

example: *Write the antecedent for each of the following adjective clauses and phrases.*

. . . that inactivate or eliminate foreign cells . . . (¶ 1)
. . . capable of an adaptive immunity . . . (¶ 5)

IV. Prediction

These subsections help students learn to save time when skimming by preparing them to read selectively. A series of exercises allows students to infer or deduce what is likely to be contained in a reading by working with thought connectors, logic, topic sentences, and outline format.

MATERIALS LESSONS (all even-numbered lessons)

Because comprehension consists of more than just reading paragraphs, these five lessons concentrate on the comprehension of the physical and visual features predictably found in published textbooks of science. Some physical ones are tables of contents, bibliographies, glossaries, reference lists, and indexes. Some illustrative or visual ones are charts, tables, diagrams, and graphs.

Throughout these even-numbered lessons, students perform hands-on comprehension tasks on unedited excerpts from real, published college-level science materials. Students learn how to use a bibliography, what information to expect to find in a preface or an introduction, and how to use the preceding and other physical features of textbooks in determining the value a particular book might have for them.

In addition, students receive concentrated practice in interpreting the tables, charts, line graphs, bar graphs, circle graphs, and schematic illustrations that are invariably encountered in all texts in all areas of specialization.

*   *   *

When students complete this volume, they should find they have a wealth of comprehension skills that will make them confident they can attack university-level materials in their individual areas of interest.

JOAN M. SASLOW

JOHN F. MONGILLO

ENGLISH IN CONTEXT

Reading Comprehension
for Science and Technology

The Retina

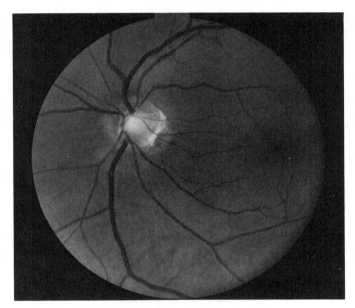

Fundus of eye

posterior: back, rear

Within the choroid, covering the posterior two-thirds of the eyeball, is the final destination of the light, the light-sensitive layer called the retina. The purpose of everything in front of the retina is ultimately to form an appropriate real image of the outside world on this layer. This image, like that of a single thin lens, **is inverted** on the retina.

focal length: the point at which rays from the left and right eye cross

accommodated: adjusted

The effective focal length of the relaxed eye is about 17 mm, which means that the retinal image is the same size as that which would be formed by a single 17 mm focal length lens. When the eye is fully accommodated for nearby objects, the effective focal length **shrinks** to about 14 mm.

Often when people first learn of the inverted retinal image, they are puzzled as to why we do not see the world upside down. However, a little contemplation **will clear up** the mystery. Seeing is **emphatically** not just the **passive transfer** of the retinal image to

From Gary Waldman, *Introduction to Light: The Physics of Light, Vision, and Color* (Englewood Cliffs, N.J.: Prentice-Hall, Inc., 1983), pp. 126–127.

1

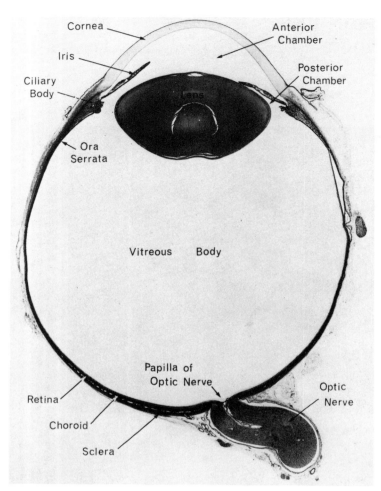

A cross-section of the eye shows its various parts.
D.W. Fawcett, Photo Researchers, Inc.

some portion of the brain for inspection by some kind of little demon there (after all, how would the demon "see" it?). The retinal image has always been inverted; usually we have had no experience of anything else. The **conscious** "picture" we see is simply the way the brain interprets the retinal image as it exists. **Along these lines**, some very interesting experiments have been done with human **subjects** wearing inverting goggles. The American psychologist G. M. Stratton actually wore an image-inverting device for 8 days as long ago as the 1890s. **As far as we know** he was the first person to see with a noninverted, or right-side-up, retinal image. Of course, ordinary actions were difficult at first, but by the fifth day things seemed almost normal although his view of parts of his own body still

2

seemed confused. When he removed the device after 8 days, the normal view of the world with inverted retinal image seemed bewildering but not **upside down**; the strangeness lasted only a few hours. **Apparently**, the visual system can learn to function with very different kinds of retinal images, even those **distorted** in more complex ways.

Nearsightedness and Farsightedness

Two common visual defects result from failure of the eye **to focus** images precisely at the position of the retina. Nearsightedness, or myopia, occurs when the eyeball is longer than normal so that the relaxed eye forms the image of a distant object in front of the retina. Farsightedness, or hyperopia, occurs when the eyeball is shorter than normal so that the relaxed eye forms the image of a distant object behind the retina. The figure below illustrates these conditions.

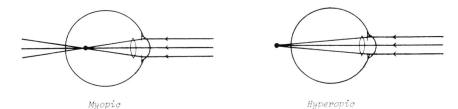

Myopic   Hyperopic

Sometimes the word hypermetropia is used in place of hyperopia. Actually the nearsighted person can see nearby things fairly clearly; we could say the myopic person's far point (the farthest away one can focus) is less than **infinity**. You can understand this result if you remember our earlier discussion of the image-forming properties of lenses; as an object is moved closer to a lens, its real image moves farther away. An object close enough to the relaxed myopic eye will produce an image on the retina, and any object closer can then be focused by accommodation. The opposite is true for the hyperopic person; distant objects can be seen clearly, but the near point is abnormally far away. In this respect the figure above is somewhat **misleading** because the eye is shown relaxed, whereas the hyperopic person would actually accommodate slightly (fatten the lens) to bring the image onto the retina. Only in this case, because of the shortness of the eyeball, full accommodation will bring into focus only things relatively far away; any closer object will be blurred. Note that both the presbyopic and hyperopic eye are characterized by abnormally distant near points and could be called farsighted, but for different reasons, **the former** because of the lens, **the latter** because of the shape of the eyeball. The nearsighted eye can be corrected by diverging lens and the farsighted eye by a converging lens.

3

blurred: not clear

diverging: separating

converging: joining

Vocabulary

to invert (verb)

> to turn so that what was originally on top becomes what is now on the bottom

> This image, like that of a single thin lens, **is inverted** on the retina.

to shrink (verb)

> to become smaller

> When the eye is fully accommodated for nearby objects, the effective focal length **shrinks** to about 14 mm.

to clear up (phrasal verb)

> to solve

> However, a little contemplation **will clear up** the mystery.

emphatically (adverb)

most surely; most definitely

Seeing is **emphatically** not just the passive transfer of the retinal image to some portion of the brain for inspection.

passive (adjective)

inactive; inert; nonparticipatory

Seeing is emphatically not just the **passive** transfer of the retinal image to some portion of the brain for inspection.

transfer (noun)

conveyance or carrying from one place to another

Seeing is emphatically not just the passive **transfer** of the retinal image to some portion of the brain for inspection.

conscious (adjective)

known

The **conscious** "picture" we see is simply the way the brain interprets the retinal image as it exists.

along these lines (thought connector)

in a similar way

Along these lines, some very interesting experiments have been done with human subjects wearing inverting goggles.

subject (noun)

person studied or observed in a medical or psychological experiment

Along these lines, some very interesting experiments have been done with human **subjects** wearing inverting goggles.

as far as we know (expression)

to the degree that we know

As far as we know he was the first person to see with a noninverted, or right-side-up, retinal image.

upside down (expression)

inverted

When he removed the device after 8 days, the normal view of the world with inverted retinal image seemed bewildering but not **upside down**.

apparently (adverb)

seemingly; evidently

Apparently, the visual system can learn to function with very different kinds of retinal images . . .

to distort (verb)

to change into an abnormal or inaccurate form

Apparently, the visual system can learn to function with very different kinds of retinal images, even those **distorted** in more complex ways.

to focus (verb)

to make an image clear by adjusting the eye or a lens

Two common visual defects result from failure of the eye **to focus** images precisely at the position of the retina.

infinity (noun)

endless distance

We could say the myopic person's far point (the farthest away one can focus) is less than **infinity**.

misleading (adjective)

causing an incorrect conclusion; leading to error

In this respect the figure above is somewhat **misleading** because the eye is shown relaxed.

the former (noun)

the earlier; the first one

Note that both the presbyopic and hyperopic eye are characterized by abnormally distant near points and could be called farsighted, but for different reasons, **the former** because of the lens, the latter because of the shape of the eyeball.

the latter (noun)

the later one; the second one

Note that both the presbyopic and hyperopic eye are characterized by abnormally distant near points and could be called farsighted, but for different reasons, the former because of the lens, **the latter** because of the shape of the eyeball.

Vocabulary Exercises

A. Complete the following statements with words from the list.

transfer	inverted	as far as we know	the latter
focused	infinity	passive	clear up
the former	distort	along these lines	

1. The airborne _____ of sulfur dioxide particles is implicated in the formation of acid rain.

2. _____ there is no life on any other planet in our solar system.

3. During space travel, weightlessness causes the astronauts to spend considerable time

   in an _____ , or upside-down, position.

4. When you take an action, you are not _____ .

5. All cameras can be _____ at various distances.

6. It is difficult to understand the concept of _____ because it is unimaginably big.

7. There has been a definite move away from invasive diagnostic techniques;

   _____ are several scanning devices that have been recently developed.

8. The wrong eyeglasses can _____ the image you see.

9. The following explanation should _____ the confusion.

A young man having the required eye test for his driver's license
Laimute E. Druskis

10. Physics and mathematics are studied in the traditional classroom;

    _____ , however, usually requires some laboratory study as well.

11. Candy and meat are both foods; of the two, however, only

    _____ is high in protein.

B. Respond T if the statement is true, or F if the statement is false.

_____ 1. If the results of an experiment are misleading, they can easily lead you to the wrong conclusion.

_____ 2. When something is stated emphatically, it is said in an unsure way.

_____ 3. If something appears to be true, it is apparently true.

_____ 4. When you stand on your feet, you are in an upside-down position.

_____ 5. A conscious thought is unknown to the thinker.

_____ 6. Something expands when it shrinks.

_____ 7. A person studied in an experiment is a subject.

Comprehension

I. Meaning

EXERCISE

C. Choose a or b to answer each numbered question. Refer to the reading on pages 1–3 as necessary.

1. What is seeing?
   a. the brain's interpretation of the image as it exists on the retina
   b. the nonparticipatory conveyance to the brain of the image on the retina

2. What is the retina?
   a. the light-sensitive layer near the back part of the eye
   b. another word for the choroid

3. How are a single thin lens and the eye's retina similar?
   a. They both receive an upside-down image.
   b. They both are mysterious.

4. Which of the following was an idea stated by the author?
   a. that myopia and hyperopia can be corrected with different lenses
   b. that age has an impact on vision

5. What does *to be puzzled* mean?
   a. to be confused; not to understand
   b. to be upside down

6. What are *goggles*?
   a. an apparatus somewhat like eyeglasses
   b. something to eat

7. What does *bewildering* mean?
   a. confusing or puzzling
   b. inverted or upside down

8. Where is the image formed by a nearsighted person?
   a. on the retina
   b. in front of the retina

9. Where is the image formed by a hypermetropic person?
   a. on the retina
   b. behind the retina

10. What is a *defect*?
    a. something good
    b. something bad

11. How does the eye focus?
    a. by relaxation
    b. by accommodation

12. What happens when an object is moved closer to the lens in the eye?
    a. Its real image moves farther away.
    b. Its near point is abnormally far away.

13. What was the purpose of G. M. Stratton's experiment?
    a. to judge the effect on the visual system of a right-side-up retinal image
    b. to wear an image-inverting device for a long period of time

14. How far does light travel in the eye?
    a. as far as the retina
    b. as far as the brain

15. What is the main subject of this selection?
    a. the retina and its role in normal vision and defective vision
    b. the use of corrective lenses in improving vision

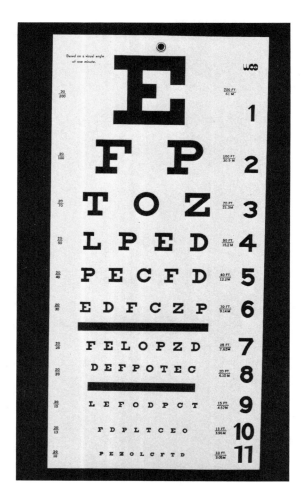

The Snellen eye chart is used to determine visual acuity.
WCO Creative Services Group

II. Reference

D. Choose a or b to indicate the reference for the italicized word or phrase in each statement taken from the reading on pages 1-3. The paragraph number is indicated to help you locate the sentence within the reading.

1. *This image*, like that of a single thin lens, is inverted on the retina. (¶ 1)
   a. an appropriate real image of the outside world
   b. that of a single thin lens

2. This image, like *that* of a single thin lens, is inverted on the retina. (¶ 1).
   a. the outside world
   b. the image

3. The effective focal length of the relaxed eye is about 17 mm, which means that the retinal image is the same size as *that* which would be formed by a single 17 mm focal length lens. (¶ 1)
   a. the retinal image
   b. the 17 mm focal length lens

4. However, a little contemplation will clear up *the mystery*. (¶ 2)
   a. why we don't see the world upside down
   b. why the image is inverted on the retina

5. Seeing is emphatically not just the passive transfer of the retinal image to some portion of the brain for inspection by some kind of demon *there* (after all, how would the demon "see" it?). (¶ 2)
   a. on the retina
   b. in the brain

6. The conscious "picture" we see is simply the way the brain interprets the retinal image as *it* exists. (¶ 2)
   a. the brain
   b. the retinal image

7. The figure below illustrates *these conditions*. (¶ 3)
   a. relaxation and accommodation
   b. nearsightedness and farsightedness

8. *The opposite* is true for the hyperopic person; distant objects can be seen clearly, but the near point is abnormally far away. (¶ 3)
   a. being able to see distant objects more clearly than close objects
   b. being able to see close objects more clearly than distant objects

9. Note that both the presbyopic and hyperopic eye are characterized by abnormally distant near points and could be called farsighted, but for different reasons, *the former* because of the lens, the latter because of the shape of the eyeball. (¶ 3)
   a. the hyperopic eye
   b. the presbyopic eye

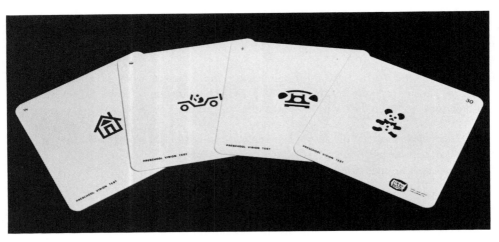

Cards used to test the vision of children who don't yet read
WCO Creative Services Group

10. Note that both the presbyopic and hyperopic eye are characterized by abnormally distant near points and could be called farsighted, but for different reasons, the former because of the lens, *the latter* because of the shape of the eyeball. (¶ 3)
   a. the hyperopic eye
   b. the shape of the eyeball

III. *Syntax: Preposed Modifying Clusters*

EXERCISE

E. Choose the paraphrase closer in meaning to each of the following phrases taken from the reading.

1. light-sensitive layer
   a. a layer that is sensitive to light
   b. light that is sensitive to layers

2. effective focal length
   a. a long focal effect
   b. a focal length that is effective

3. a single 17 mm focal length lens
   a. a single lens with a 17 mm focal length
   b. a 17 mm lens with a single focal length

4. an image-inverting device
   a. an image that inverts devices
   b. a device that inverts images

5. a noninverted, or right-side-up retinal image
   a. an image that is noninverted, right-side-up, and retinal
   b. a retinal image that is noninverted or right-side-up

6. an inverted retinal image
   a. a retinal image that is inverted
   b. a retina that is inverted and imaged

7. image-forming properties
   a. properties that form images
   b. images that form properties

8. abnormally distant near points
   a. distant near points that are abnormal
   b. near points that are abnormally distant

COMPREHENSION SKILL INDEX

Prediction: Thought Connectors

A helpful reading skill is the ability to predict what will come next in a narrative. This skill will sometimes make it possible for you to understand the idea contained in a sentence or an entire paragraph even when it contains many unknown words. One way to predict what is to come is to make use of thought connectors. You already know the literal meaning of most of these important words and phrases.

Study the following groups of thought connectors, paying attention to what each group predicts.

Predict That Additional Information Will Follow

along these lines	furthermore
and	in addition (additionally)
and also	in this respect
and . . . to	moreover
as well as	not just
besides	not only

examples: Sharks have an exceptionally keen sense of smell. *And* it has been recently discovered that they have excellent sight.

Traditional retinal reattachment surgery is expensive, is time-consuming, and requires a hospital stay. *Besides*, it carries the risk of operative complications.

Predict That a Result or an Outcome Will Follow

accordingly	hence
as a consequence	so that
as a result	therefore
consequently	thus

examples: It has been observed that high salt consumption is linked to hypertension. *Consequently*, most clinicians advise patients to lower sodium intake to mitigate this risk.

Robots have many advantages over human workers in many settings. *Therefore*, their use is being expanded wherever appropriate.

Predict That a Contrasting Statement Will Follow

all the same	in spite of the fact that
although	nevertheless
but	only
even so	still
even though	whereas
however	yet

examples: X-ray machines can perform many noninvasive diagnostic procedures requiring a view of bone or other opaque structures. *Nevertheless*, they are limited because they cannot show most soft tissues.

Most sharks are quite harmless *even though* they are almost universally feared.

IV. *Prediction: Thought Connectors*

EXERCISE

F. Predict whether the following words will present an addition, a result, or a contrast. The sentences are taken from the reading on pages 1–3. Paragraph numbers are indicated.

1. Often when people first learn of the inverted retinal image, they are puzzled as to why we do not see the world upside down. *However* . . . (¶ 2)

   (_____)

2. Seeing is emphatically *not just* the passive transfer of the retinal image to some portion of the brain for inspection by some kind of little demon there (after all, how would the demon "see" it?) . . . (¶ 2) (_____)

3. The conscious "picture" we see is simply the way the brain interprets the retinal image as it exists. *Along these lines* . . . (¶ 2) (_____)

4. Of course, ordinary actions were difficult at first, but by the fifth day things seemed almost normal *although* . . . (¶ 2) (_____)

5. Of course, ordinary actions were difficult at first, *but* . . . (¶ 2)

   (_____)

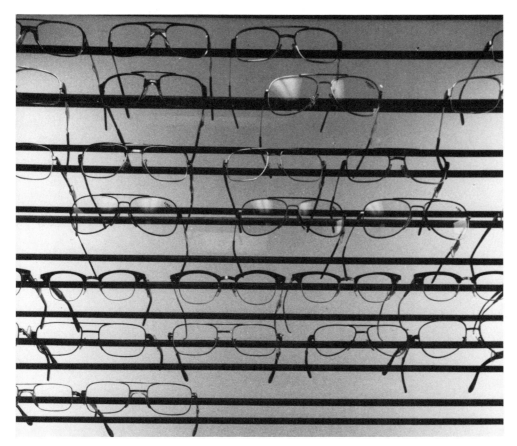

A display of eyeglass frames at the optometrist's office
Laimute E. Druskis

6. When he removed the device after 8 days, the normal view of the world with inverted retinal image seemed bewildering *but* . . . (¶ 2)

(_____)

7. Nearsightedness, or myopia, occurs when the eyeball is longer than normal *so that* . . . (¶ 3) (_____)

8. An object close enough to the relaxed myopic eye will produce an image on the retina, *and* . . . (¶ 3) (_____)

9. The opposite is true for the hyperopic person; distant objects can be seen clearly, *but* . . . (¶ 3) (_____)

10. . . . distant objects can be seen clearly, but the near point is abnormally far away. *In this respect* . . . (¶ 3) (_____)

11. In this respect the figure above is somewhat misleading because the eye is shown relaxed, *whereas* . . . (¶ 3) (_____)

12. . . . the hyperopic person would actually accommodate slightly (fatten the lens) to bring the image onto the retina. *Only* . . . (¶ 3) (_____)

13. Note that both the presbyopic and hyperopic eye are characterized by abnormally distant near points and could be called farsighted, *but* . . . (¶ 3)

(_____)

LESSON TWO
Materials

Textbook Features

Science textbooks and technical and professional journals are usually made up of several parts and contain various special features, many of which have a standard format. Textbooks usually contain a large number of these parts; journals and manuals contain many, but not all of them.

Knowing where to look for information and what to expect in a book can greatly increase your ability to use all the information there. Explanations of and practice using some of these textbook parts and features are covered in these even-numbered lessons. The features in textbooks are grouped into the following three categories. *Front matter* is the roman-numeral paginated section at the front of most books. The *text* is the main body of the book. The *back matter* comprises the additional sections at the back of most books. Although our discussion of these three sections will deal mainly with textbooks, the practice provided will greatly enhance your comprehension of scientific journals as well.

Front Matter	Main Text
title page	introductions
copyright page	running head
preface	running foot
table of contents	illustrations and captions
"to the student"	display copy
"to the instructor"	headnotes
illustration lists	footnotes
	conclusion/summary
	typography to indicate structure and hierarchy
	internal numbering sequence
	suggested readings

Back Matter	Other
appendix (data tables, reference lists, etc.)	endpapers
footnotes	
bibliography	
references	
glossary	
index	

Very few books contain all these parts, and you will sometimes find additional parts that are not listed here. The first half of each even-numbered lesson in this book will be devoted to helping you get the most out of these parts and features.

Title Page

The first or second (rarely, the third) right-hand page of a hardcover book is the title page. A softcover workbook, lab manual, technical pamphlet or manual, or a journal often uses the cover itself as the title page. Occasionally, in order to fill additional pages, a half-title page precedes the title page on the right-hand page immediately before the title page. A half-title page does not contain all the information the title page does. Also, occasionally, when there is a half-title page, the title page is designed as a two-page spread on the left- and right-hand pages following it.

The title page is in some ways the most important page in the book. It is the place where the official information about a book is found. It is this page that provides libraries and researchers the full title of the book and the full name(s) of the author(s). Following is a list of what you can expect to find on the title page.

1. Title: the name of the book or journal.

   example: English in Context

2. Subtitle (if any).

   example: Reading Comprehension for Science and Technology

3. Author's name (authors' names) or editor's name. When it is appropriate, you may find the name of a translator or other important contributor to the work.

   example: Joan M. Saslow

   John F. Mongillo

4. Name of the publishing house, academic institution, or professional society that published the work.

   example: Prentice-Hall

In addition, you may find the following: edition number (of a previously published work); city or cities in which the publisher has an office; series title and volume number of a multivolume work. You may find other information as well. Keep in mind, though, that you will always find the title, the author's name, and the name of the publishing house on the title page.

Title Page

EXERCISE

A. Find the title page of this book and look at it. Respond T if the statement is true, F if the statement is false, or ? if the information cannot be learned from looking at the title page.

_____ 1. The book has no subtitle.

_____ 2. The full title of the book is *Reading Comprehension for Science and Technology*.

_____ 3. The book was published in 1984.

_____ 4. The book is probably a first edition.

_____ 5. The book ends on page 183.

_____ 6. The publisher is not mentioned.

_____ 7. The title page is the first right-hand page.

_____ 8. There are two authors of this book.

_____ 9. The book is the third book of a series.

_____ 10. The authors have advanced degrees.

Copyright Page

The copyright page is virtually always found on the first left-hand page after the title page. If the cover serves as the title page, the inside front cover will be the copyright page. This frequently happens with workbooks, lab manuals, and other softcover books. The copyright page contains the following information.

1. Copyright notice. This indicates who owns the copyright and the year in which the book or journal was published.

    example: Copyright © 1986 by Prentice-Hall, Inc. Englewood Cliffs, New Jersey

2. Country in which the book was printed (occasionally found elsewhere in the book).

    example: Printed in the United States of America

3. International Standard Book Number (ISBN) or ISSN for serial publications. This number is an identifying number.

    example: 0-13-280041-1

In addition, some or all of the following may be included on the copyright page. These elements vary in form from publisher to publisher, and it is unlikely that you will find all of them on any one copyright page.

4. Expanded (or full) copyright notice.

    example: All rights reserved.
    No part of this book may be reproduced
    in any form or by any means
    without permission in writing from the publisher.

5. Library of Congress CIP (Cataloging in Publication) data. This helps librarians place the book on the shelves quickly because the cataloging has already been done for them.

example: **Library of Congress Cataloging in Publication Data**

La Place, John.
Health.

Bibliography: pp. 538–45.
Includes index.
1. Health. 2. Public health. I. Title. [DNLM:
1. Health. 2. Public health. WA 4 L312h]
RA776.L348 1983   613   83-17714
ISBN   0-13-385435-3

6. History of the work. This is often in the form of a chronological list of the dates of prior editions and/or printings.

example: First Printing, 1974
Second Printing, 1975

7. Printing impression line. This shows the printing number and sometimes the date of that printing. The following indicates a fifth printing.

example: Printed in the United States of America.

10 9 8 7 6 5

8. Publisher's address.

example: Mayfield Publishing Company
285 Hamilton Avenue
Palo Alto, California 94301

9. Permissions. This listing, when included, indicates the source and copyright owner of material quoted within the book.

example: **Credits**

Page 4 From *San Francisco Examiner*, November 24, 1980. Reprinted with permission.
Pages 8, 12, 13 From the book *Become an Ex-Smoker* by Brian G. Danaher & Edward Lichtenstein. Copyright © 1978 by Prentice-Hall, Inc. Published by Prentice-Hall, Inc., Englewood Cliffs, N.J. 07632.
Pages 19, 52 L. John Mason, *Guide to Stress Reduction* (Culver City, Calif.: Peace Press, 1980). Copyright © 1980 L. John Mason, Ph.D.
Page 27 Reprinted by permission; copyright © 1981 The New Yorker Magazine, Inc.
Page 36 THE LIBRARY OF HEALTH, *Stress* by Ogden Tanner and the Editors of Time-Life Books; copyright © 1976 Time Inc.

10. Photo credits. This listing acknowledges the owners of photos used in the book.

example:

Photo Credits:
Cover: Bicycling Magazine/Sally Shenk Ullman
Title Page: Jim Anderson, Woodfin Camp & Associates
Chapter Openings: Introduction: Bill Strode, Woodfin Camp & Associates; 1: Charles
Gatewood; 2: Richard Falo, Photo Researchers, Inc.; 3: Jim Anderson, Woodfin Camp &
Associates; 4: Laimute E. Druskis; 5: Joel Gordon; 6: Suzanne Szasz, Photo Researchers, Inc.;
7: Frank Siteman, Stock, Boston; 8: Ken Karp; 9: Ken Karp; 10: Owen Franken, Stock, Boston;
11: John C. Pitkin; 12: Amy Meadow; 13: Chris Maynard, Stock, Boston; 14: Ken Karp;
15: Ken Karp; 16: F. Botts, United Nations

Copyright Page

EXERCISES

B. Find the copyright page for this book and look at it. In the following list, circle the number of the elements you find there.

1. copyright symbol
2. copyright date
3. authors' names
4. printing impression line
5. CIP data
6. publishing history
7. photo credits
8. permissions
9. country in which the book was printed
10. full copyright notice
11. copyright owner
12. publisher's address
13. ISBN

C. Look at the copyright page of a large science textbook. Give the following information, if it is included. If it is not included on the copyright page, write *not included*.

1. Publisher's address _____

2. Copyright date _____

3. Dates of prior editions _____

4. Full copyright notice _____

_____

_____

5. Printing impression line _____

6. ISBN _____

7. Place where the book was printed _____

8. Copyright owner _____

D. List any other elements found on the textbook copyright page you are looking at.

_____

_____

_____

Table of Contents

Virtually all textbooks, scientific journals, and technical manuals have a table of contents. The table of contents is usually called "Contents." Although tables of contents differ significantly in the degree of their completeness, they are always arranged sequentially, giving you an overall outline of what the work contains. In most textbooks you will find the following.

1. Title of each section or chapter of the book.
2. Page number on which each section or chapter begins.
3. Title of each major part of the book, if the chapters are grouped into major parts.
4. Subsections of chapters or major parts (if these exist and the publisher had space to include them).
5. Page number on which each section of front and back matter begins.
6. Page numbers on which exercises occur (in very complete tables of contents).

Table of Contents

EXERCISES

E. Find the table of contents of this book and, as you refer to it, mark the following statements true (T) or false (F).

_____ 1. The book is divided into ten lessons.

_____ 2. There are two different types of lesson.

_____ 3. Each lesson begins with the same element.

_____ 4. The table of contents is organized alphabetically.

_____ 5. A glossary is included in this book.

_____ 6. Lesson Six begins on page 93.

_____ 7. Vocabulary is a part of each lesson.

_____ 8. The table of contents contains acknowledgment of permissions to use excerpts from other books.

_____ 9. The table of contents tells you the page this book ends on.

F. Look at the following complex and unusually complete table of contents and refer to it in answering the following questions. Note that this table of contents contains a few infrequently used features, such as the previews.

1. How many chapters is the book divided into? _____

2. How many parts is Chapter 19 divided into? _____

3. What chapter would you go to to read about the applications of Newton's Laws?

_____

4. In which chapter would you find a comparison of the Celsius and Fahrenheit scales?

_____

5. After the general introduction to physics covered in Chapters 1–9, what major area of physics is covered in Chapters 10-14? _____

_____

6. What major area of physics is covered in Chapters 29–46? _____

_____

7. What are two features included at the end of almost all chapters? _____

_____

8. What features are found in the back matter? _____

_____

9. What features are found in the front matter? _____

_____

10. What is the first feature of most chapters (after the title)? _____

_____

CONTENTS

From Sheldon H. Radin and Robert T. Folk, *Physics for Scientists and Engineers*
(Englewood Cliffs, N.J.: Prentice-Hall, Inc., 1982), pp. v-xi.

Reading and Interpreting Charts, Tables, Diagrams, Graphs, Line Drawings, and Schematic Illustrations

In addition to the narrative prose that has been the core of the material presented so far, scientific and technical writing makes frequent use of illustrations in the form of charts, tables, graphs, line drawings, and schematic illustrations. Each even-numbered lesson in this text will include a section on reading and interpreting these high-frequency features of the books and journals you wish to read.

Writers use charts, tables, graphs, and other illustrations to help explain the ideas they are writing about. These features are highly important and never serve as mere decorations. Sometimes, in fact, it is impossible to read or understand the narrative without using the accompanying illustration.

Tables

Tables show comparisons in vertical columns. Writers use them in order to save space, because a lot of information can be presented on a table. If each bit of information were conveyed in a separate sentence, the information contained in a simple table could cover several pages. In addition to permitting the author to save space, tables are very convenient for the reader, who can see the comparisons immediately and quickly since only essential information is included in the table. The visual impact of a table is one of its most valuable features.

Certain procedures need to be followed whenever you read a table. Be sure you understand the meaning of each part of the table by following the steps below. Look up any words in the table you cannot guess.

1. Read the title of the table (either above or below the table—usually in larger or darker type than other text). This tells you what information you will find in the table.
2. Read subtitles at the top of the columns. These tell you what information each column contains and what kind of units it is presented in (such as percentages, dates, money, etc.).

3. Read any other information that occurs along the bottom and sides of the table. This information may be in the form of footnotes which explain the data in some essential way; it may be a statement of the source of the data or of the table itself, which would help you evaluate the reliability of the information; it may be the date that the information was collected, which would help you determine whether the information is valid today.

4. Read two lines across (horizontally) to make sure you know what you are reading. Reading these two lines helps you see the comparison that the table is presenting. If you are still unsure about the purpose and meaning of the table, review steps 1 to 3. Knowing the purpose and meaning of the table will tell you whether or not the information is essential to your purposes.

Tables

EXERCISES

Table 1.2 Composition of the Atmosphere

	Per cent	Partial pressure (mm Hg)
Oxygen	20.948	159.20
Carbon dioxide	0.030[1]	0.23
Nitrogen	78.00	592.8
Argon	0.94	7.15
Other	0.082	0.62

SOURCE: Krogh, 1941: The Comparative Physiology of Respiratory Mechanisms. University of Pennsylvania Press, Philadelphia.
[1]May rise to about 0.04 per cent in streets of large cities and is increasing significantly during this century because of the burning of fossil fuels and greater agricultural activities (Baes *et al.*, 1977; Woodwell, 1978).

From William S. Hoar, *General and Comparative Physiology* (Englewood Cliffs, N.J.: Prentice-Hall, Inc., 1983), p. 27.

G. Refer to the table above in choosing the best answer to the following questions.

1. What information is presented in the table?
    a. comparative physiology of respiratory mechanisms
    b. components of the atmosphere
2. In what form are the relative amounts of each gas presented?
    a. weight
    b. percent

3. In what other units are these gases compared?
   a. millimeters of mercury
   b. partial pressure

4. Who was the source of the information?
   a. Krogh
   b. Woodwell

5. What is happening to the percentage of carbon dioxide in the atmosphere of cities?
   a. It is declining.
   b. It is rising.

6. What is the effect of fossil fuel combustion on the composition of the atmosphere?
   a. It reduces the amount of carbon dioxide in the air.
   b. It increases the amount of carbon dioxide in the air.

7. What percentage of the atmosphere is made up of oxygen?
   a. 159.20
   b. 20.948

8. What is the most abundant gas in the atmosphere?
   a. nitrogen
   b. oxygen

9. What other components make up the atmosphere?
   a. none
   b. It is impossible to know from this table.

H. Refer to the table on pages 36 and 37 to answer the following questions.
   1. What are the names of three depressant drugs? _____

   _____

   2. What is the brand name of methylphenidate? _____

   _____

   3. What are two medical uses of codeine? _____

   _____

   4. What is the physical dependence potential of heroin? _____

   _____

   5. What is the psychological dependence potential of Preludin? _____

   _____

   6. What is the duration of the effects of most tranquilizers? _____

   _____

7. By what method is chloral hydrate administered? _____

_____

8. What are two possible effects of amphetamines? _____

_____

9. Which categories of controlled substances can result in death when taken in over-dose quantities? _____

10. Which category of controlled substances has no apparent withdrawal syndrome?

_____

TABLE 18-7   Controlled substances of both natural and synthetic origin.

Drugs		Often-Prescribed Brand Names	Medical Uses	Dependence Potential: Physical
Narcotics	Opium	Dover's Powder, Paregoric	Analgesic, antidiarrheal	High
	Morphine	Morphine	Analgesic	High
	Codeine	Codeine	Analgesic, antitussive	Moderate
	Heroin	None	None	High
	Meperidine (Pethidine)	Demerol, Pethadol	Analgesic	High
	Methadone	Dolophine, Methadone, Methadose	Analgesic, heroin substitute	High
	Other Narcotics	Dilaudid, Leritine, Numorphan, Percodan	Analgesic, antidiarrheal, antitussive	High
Depressants	Chloral Hydrate	Noctec, Somnos	Hypnotic	Moderate
	Barbiturates	Amytal, Butisol, Nembutal, Phenobarbital, Seconal, Tuinal	Anesthetic, anti-convulsant, sedation, sleep	High
	Glutethimide	Doriden	Sedation, sleep	High
	Methaqualone	Optimil, Parest, Quaalude, Somnafac, Sopor	Sedation, sleep	High
	Tranquilizers	Equanil, Librium, Miltown Serax, Tranxene, Valium	Anti-anxiety, muscle relaxant, sedation	Moderate
	Other Depressants	Clonopin, Dalmane, Dormate, Noludar, Placydil, Valmid	Anti-anxiety, sedation, sleep	Possible
Stimulants	Cocaine[a]	Cocaine	Local anesthetic	Possible
	Amphetamines	Benzedrine, Biphetamine, Desoxyn, Dexedrine	Hyperkinesis, narcolepsy, weight control	Possible
	Phenmetrazine	Preludin	Weight control	Possible
	Methylphenidate	Ritalin	Hyperkinesis	Possible
	Other Stimulants	Bacarate, Cylert, Didrex, Ionamin, Plegine, Pondimin, Pre-Sate, Sanorex, Voranil	Weight control	Possible
Hallucinogens	LSD	None	None	None
	Mescaline	None	None	None
	Psilocybin-Psilocyn	None	None	None
	MDA	None	None	None
	PCP[b]	Sernylan	Veterinary anesthetic	None
	Other Hallucinogens	None	None	None
Cannabis	Marihuana Hashish Hashish Oil	None	None	Degree unknown

[a]Designated a narcotic under the Controlled Substances Act.
[b]Designated a depressant under the Controlled Substances Act.
Adapted from *Drugs of Abuse,* 3rd ed., U.S. Department of Justice, Drug Enforcement Administration.

From Roy H. Saigo and Barbara W. Saigo, *Botany: Principles and Applications* (Englewood Cliffs, N.J.: Prentice-Hall, Inc., 1983), pp. 454-455.

Dependence Potential: Psychological	Tolerance	Duration of Effects (in hours)	Usual Methods of Administration	Possible Effects	Effects of Overdose	Withdrawal Syndrome
High	Yes	3–6	Oral, smoked	Euphoria, drowsiness, respiratory depression, constricted pupils, nausea	Slow and shallow breathing, clammy skin, convulsions, coma, possible death	Watery eyes, runny nose, yawning, loss of appetite, irritability, tremors, panic, chills and sweating, cramps, nausea
High	Yes	3–6	Injected, smoked			
Moderate	Yes	3–6	Oral, injected			
High	Yes	3–6	Injected, sniffed			
High	Yes	3–6	Oral, injected			
High	Yes	12–24	Oral, injected			
High	Yes	3–6	Oral, injected			
Moderate	Probable	5–8	Oral	Slurred speech, disorientation, drunken behavior without odor of alcohol	Shallow respiration, cold and clammy skin, dilated pupils, weak and rapid pulse, coma, possible death	Anxiety, insomnia, tremors, delirium, convulsions, possible death
High	Yes	1–16	Oral, injected			
High	Yes	4–8	Oral			
High	Yes	4–8	Oral			
Moderate	Yes	4–8	Oral			
Possible	Yes	4–8	Oral			
High	Yes	2	Injected, sniffed	Increased alertness, excitation, euphoria, dilated pupils, increased pulse rate and blood pressure, insomnia, loss of appetite	Agitation, increase in body temperature, hallucinations, convulsions, possible death	Apathy, long periods of sleep, irritability, depression, disorientation
High	Yes	2–4	Oral, injected			
High	Yes	2–4	Oral			
High	Yes	2–4	Oral			
Possible	Yes	2–4	Oral			
Degree unknown	Yes	Variable	Oral	Illusions and hallucinations (with exception of MDA); poor perception of time and distance	Longer, more intense "trip" episodes, psychosis, possible death	Withdrawal syndrome not reported
Degree unknown	Yes	Variable	Oral, injected			
Degree unknown	Yes	Variable	Oral			
Degree unknown	Yes	Variable	Oral, injected, sniffed			
Degree unknown	Yes	Variable	Oral, injected, smoked			
Degree unknown	Yes	Variable	Oral, injected, sniffed			
Moderate	Yes	2–4	Oral, smoked	Euphoria, relaxed inhibitions, increased appetite, disoriented behavior	Fatigue, paranoia, possible psychosis	Insomnia, hyperactivity, and decreased appetite reported in a limited number of individuals

Charts

Charts are often included in textbooks and journals to serve as a reference source for information mentioned in the narrative. Information is arranged in vertical columns similar to those in tables. However, the purpose of the arrangement is not usually comparison but rather brevity of reference or giving of instructions. The following charts illustrate the two major uses of this feature.

charts for brevity

Acronyms and abbreviations

a	ampere, unit of current OR op amp open loop gain	F	farad, unit of capacitance
AC	alternating (oscillatory) current or voltage	FET	field-effect transistor
		FF	flip flop
A/D or		FG	function generator
ADC	analog to digital converter	FIFO	first in, first out
AM	amplitude modulation	FLAG	device status signal (ready/not ready)
AND, OR	gates which perform logic AND/OR function		
		FM	frequency modulation
BIN	binary (base 2)	FS	full scale
BCD	binary-coded decimal	FSK	frequency-shift keying
BiFET	bipolar plus field-effect transistors on the same IC	FT	Fourier transform
		GND	ground connection
BiMOS	bipolar plus MOS transistors on the same IC	H	henry, unit of inductance
		HEX	hexadecimal (base 16)
BP	band-pass	HP	high-pass
C	a capacitor	Hz	hertz, unit of frequency (= cycles/sec)
CCD	charge-coupled device		
CLK	clock	IC	integrated circuit
CMOS	complementary (both p-channel and n-channel) MOS	I_{co}	reverse-bias transistor leakage current
CMRR	common mode rejection ratio	I/O	input/output
CNTL	control	Im	imaginary part of a complex number
CNTR	counter		
CPU	central processing unit	JFET	junction field-effect transistor
CS	chip-select	JK	type of flip flop with no disallowed states
CV/CC	constant voltage/constant current		
D	data or data input	L	an inductor
D/A or		LP	low pass
DAC	digital to analog converter	LSB	least significant bit
dB	decibel	LSI	large-scale integration
DC	direct (nonoscillatory) current or voltage	MOS	metal-oxide semiconductor
		MOSFET	metal-oxide-semiconductor field-effect transmitter
DMM	digital multimeter		
DMPX	demultiplex	MPU	microprocessor unit
DTL	diode-transistor logic; made obsolete by TTL	MPX	multiplex
		MPY	multiplier
DVM	digital voltmeter	MS	master–slave type of flip flop
ECL	emitter-coupled logic	MSB	most significant bit
EEPROM	electrically erasable PROM	MSI	medium-scale integration
EPROM	erasable programable read-only memory	NAND, NOR	AND/OR gates with inverted outputs

From Richard J. Higgins, *Electronics with Digital and Analog Integrated Circuits* (Englewood Cliffs, N.J.: Prentice-Hall, Inc., 1983).

NF	noise figure	S/H or SH	sample and hold
OC	open circuit	SIPO	serial in, parallel out
OCT	octal (base 8)	SISO	serial in, serial out
Ω	ohm, unit of resistance	S/N	signal to noise
op amp	operational amplifier	SPDT	single pole, double throw 2-position switch
OS	one shot (monostable multivibrator)	SR	shift register (sometimes, set-reset flip flop)
OTA	operational transconductance amplifier	STROBE	timing signal in handshaking
PIPO	parallel in, parallel out	SW	switch
PISO	parallel in, serial out	SYNC	synchronization
PLL	phase-locked loop	TG	transmission gate
p-p	peak-to-peak	TRIG	trigger or device activation
PROM	programable read-only memory	TRI-STATE	tri-state logic: high, low or disconnected
PSD	phase-sensitive detector = lock-in		
Q	quality factor, of an inductor or band pass filter	TTL	transistor–transistor logic (bipolar)
R	a resistor	UART	universal asynchronous receiver-transmitter
RAM	random access memory (volatile, in current usage)	V	volts, unit of voltage
RDY	ready	V_{cc}	collector power supply voltage
RE	real part of a complex number	VCG	voltage-controlled gain
Ref	reference: stable source of voltage or current	VCO	voltage-controlled oscillator
		V_{dd}	drain power supply voltage
RF	radio frequency range (~ 0.5 MHz and above)	V/F	voltage-to-frequency converter
		VOM	volt-ohm-meter
rms	root mean square	VTVM	vacuum tube voltmeter (obsolete)
ROM	read-only memory	WR	write
SC	short circuit	M	multiplier
SCOPE	oscilloscope	X	multiplier
SCR	silicon controlled rectifier	XOR	exclusive or gate
SEL	select		

Abbreviations of size or scale

10^{-3}	m milli-	10^{+3}	K kilo-
10^{-6}	μ micro-	10^{+6}	M mega-
10^{-9}	n nano-	10^{+9}	G giga-
10^{-12}	p pico-	10^{+12}	T tera-
10^{-15}	f femto-		

APPENDIX

Metric Conversion Chart

	Into Metric			Out of Metric	
If You Know	*Multiply By*	*To Get*	*If You Know*	*Multiply By*	*To Get*
LENGTH					
inches	2.54	centimeters	millimeters	0.04	inches
feet	30	centimeters	centimeters	0.4	inches
feet	0.303	meters	meters	3.3	feet
yards	0.91	meters	kilometers	0.62	miles
miles	1.6	kilometers			
AREA					
sq. inches	6.5	sq. centimeters	sq. centimeters	0.16	sq. inches
sq. feet	0.09	sq. meters	sq. meters	1.2	sq. yards
sq. yards	0.8	sq. meters	sq. kilometers	0.4	sq. miles
sq. miles	2.6	sq. kilometers	hectares	2.47	acres
acres	0.4	hectares			
MASS (WEIGHT)					
ounces	28	grams	grams	0.035	ounces
pounds	0.45	kilograms	kilograms	2.2	pounds
short ton	0.9	metric ton	metric tons	1.1	short tons
VOLUME					
teaspoons	5	milliliters	milliliters	0.03	fluid ounces
tablespoons	15	milliliters	liters	2.1	pints
fluid ounces	30	milliliters	liters	1.06	quarts
cups	0.24	liters	liters	0.26	gallons
pints	0.47	liters	cubic meters	35	cubic feet
quarts	0.95	liters	cubic meters	1.3	cubic yards
gallons	3.8	liters			
cubic feet	0.03	cubic meters			
cubic yards	0.76	cubic meters			
PRESSURE					
lbs/in^2	0.069	bars	bars	14.5	lbs/in^2
atmospheres	1.013	bars	bars	0.987	atmospheres
atmospheres	1.033	kg/cm^2	kg/cm^2	0.968	atmospheres
lbs/in^2	0.07	kg/cm^2	kg/cm^2	14.22	lbs/in^2
RATES					
lbs/acre	1.12	kg/hectare	kg/hectare	0.892	lbs/acre
tons/acre	2.24	metric tons/hectare	metric tons/hectare	0.445	tons/acre

From Roy H. Saigo and Barbara W. Saigo, *Botany: Principles and Applications* (Englewood Cliffs, N.J.: Prentice-Hall, Inc., 1983), p. 505.

Charts

I. Refer to the charts on pages 38-40 to respond true (T) or false (F) to the following statements.

_____ 1. BiFET is an acronym for bipolar plus field-effect transistors on the same IC.

_____ 2. An abbreviation for master-slave type of flip flop is MSB.

_____ 3. To convert grams to ounces, you multiply by 28.

_____ 4. You can use this metric conversion chart to convert Fahrenheit to Celsius.

_____ 5. One meter is 3.3 feet.

_____ 6. A short ton is the same as a metric ton.

_____ 7. To convert inches to centimeters, you multiply the number of inches by 2.54.

Root Pressure and Guttation

Guttation water on strawberry leaves

Root pressure refers to positive hydrostatic pressure that sometimes develops in the xylem sap of roots. The phenomenon can be demonstrated **readily** in the laboratory. A short piece of rubber tubing is attached to the stump of a freshly decapitated, young, well-watered herbaceous plant plotted in well aerated soil. A glass tube **is** attached to the rubber tubing and **secured** in a vertical position. The level of xylem sap in the glass tube will rise slowly in a few hours.   **1**

The first recorded demonstration and measurement of root pressure were carried out by the Englishman Stephen Hales, an early experimental plant physiologist (Hales, 1727), Root pressures are usually in the range of +1 to +2 bars, but slightly higher values have been recorded.   **2**

Root pressure is an osmotic phenomenon. Transport of mineral ions across a root gives rise to a slightly higher solute concentration

From G. Ray Noggle and George J. Fritz, *Introductory Plant Physiology*, 2nd ed. (Englewood Cliffs, N.J.: Prentice-Hall, Inc., 1983), pp. 412–413.

The arrowhead is a leafy plant.
© Lynwood M. Chase, National Audubon Society

in xylem sap than in the external soil solution. The difference in solute potential between the external soil solution and the xylem sap in a root that exhibits root pressure is the **driving force** for the movement of water across the root. 3

Root pressures have been found to fluctuate in a rhythm of small **amplitude** with a period of about 24 hours. This diurnal rhythm **persists** even if a decapitated plant is placed in a growth chamber in which environmental conditions (e.g., temperature, light, humidity) are held constant. Rhythms in biological processes (e.g., root pressure) are **due** to rhythms in protoplasmic activity—and these are reflected in changes in the **properties** of protoplasmic membranes. But the fundamental nature of biological rhythms has **yet to be determined** (see Chapter 18). 4

The volume of xylem sap **exuded** from the stump of a detopped **viable** root system is relatively small and only a fraction of the water that would be lost by the (**intact**) plant by transpiration during the same period of time. 5

Root pressure is generally regarded as having little importance in the life of most higher plants. If it has any role at all, it is only in very young plants, before leaves are developed and before transpiration becomes a **dominant** feature in the overall water economy of the plant. As we saw earlier, transpiration accounts for the absorption of water by most species of higher plants during their adult lives.

6

The development of root pressure in an intact plant **becomes** visibly **manifested** in guttation. Guttation refers to the exudation of droplets of liquid water from the **margins** and **tips** of leaves. Guttation water is exuded from groups of leaf cells called hydathodes. Typically a hydathode is an opening or pore in the leaf epidermis, around which are grouped several thin-walled parenchyma cells. Frequently the pore of a hydathode is an incompletely differentiated stoma incapable of opening and closing movements.

7

Guttation depends on root pressure. The development of root pressure in a plant leads to positive hydrostatic pressure in the xylem sap throughout the plant. Because water-conducting xylem elements of a vascular **bundle** terminate in a hydathode, xylem sap is forced to flow through the hydathode. Thus guttation water is exuded from the leaf.

8

To demonstrate guttation in the laboratory, a potted, well-watered, herbaceous plant, preferably one that is young and growing vigorously, is placed on a flat surface and covered with a bell jar. The **rim** of the bell jar **is sealed** (e.g., with petrolatum) to ensure that loss of water by transpiration is **negligible**. In a few hours guttation water will appear on the leaves.

9

Guttation water contains small amounts of both organic and inorganic solutes. The presence of organic solutes can be explained by **leakage** from cells that border on the xylem tissue. The inorganic solutes are mostly those absorbed by roots from the soil solution and carried passively to leaves in the upward-flowing xylem sap.

10

The concentration of inorganic solutes in guttation water is much smaller than in xylem sap that exudes from the rooted stump of a decapitated plant. This reduction in solute concentration is due to the fact that leaf cells absorb most of the dissolved salts passing through their xylem tissues. The small amounts of inorganic solutes present in guttation water represent the remnants of dissolved salts not removed during their passage through leaves. Thus leaf cells may be **said to be** very effective but less than perfect demineralizers.

11

Vocabulary

readily (adverb)

easily, quickly

The phenomenon can be demonstrated **readily** in the laboratory.

to secure (verb)

>to attach very firmly or permanently

>A glass tube **is** attached to the rubber tubing and **secured** in a vertical position.

driving force (expression)

>the cause

>The difference in solute potential between the external soil solution and the xylem sap in a root that exhibits root pressure is the **driving force** for the movement of water across the root.

amplitude (noun)

>range; size

>Root pressures have been found to fluctuate in a rhythm of small **amplitude** with a period of about 24 hours.

to persist (verb)

>to remain in existence; to last

>This diurnal rhythm **persists** even if a decapitated plant is placed in a growth chamber in which environmental conditions (e.g., temperature, light, humidity) are held constant.

due to (expression)

>because of; caused by

>Rhythms in biological processes (e.g., root pressure) are **due to** rhythms in protoplasmic activity.

property (noun)

>characteristic trait or quality

>Rhythms in biological processes (e.g., root pressure) are due to rhythms in protoplasmic activity—and these are reflected in changes in the **properties** of protoplasmic membranes.

yet to be determined (expression)

>still unknown or undiscovered

>But the fundamental nature of biological rhythms has **yet to be determined**.

to exude (verb)

> to emit slowly; to release; to give off

> The volume of xylem sap **exuded** from the stump of a detopped viable root system is relatively small . . .

viable (adjective)

> capable of survival; alive

> The volume of xylem sap exuded from the stump of a detopped **viable** root system is relatively small . . .

intact (adjective)

> whole; having all parts

> The volume of xylem sap exuded from the stump of a detopped viable root system is relatively small and only a fraction of the water that would be lost by the (**intact**) plant by transpiration during the same period of time.

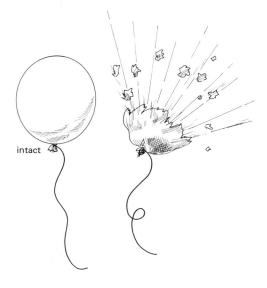

intact

dominant (adjective)

> strong; very or most important

> If it has any role at all, it is only in very young plants, before leaves are developed and before transpiration becomes a **dominant** feature in the overall water economy of the plant.

to manifest (verb)

> to show; to exhibit

> The development of root pressure in an intact plant **becomes** visibly **manifested** in guttation.

margin (noun)

> side; edge

> Guttation refers to the exudation of droplets of liquid water from the **margins** and tips of leaves.

margin

tip (noun)

> end; pointed end

> Guttation refers to the exudation of droplets of liquid water from the margins and **tips** of leaves.

tip

bundle (noun)

group of objects held together

Because water-conducting xylem elements of a vascular **bundle** terminate in a hydathode, xylem sap is forced to flow through the hydathode.

a bundle of clothes

rim (noun)

round, open edge of an object

The **rim** of the bell jar is sealed . . .

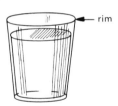

rim

to seal (verb)

to close tight, sometimes by means of a substance that doesn't let air or liquid pass

The rim of the bell jar **is sealed** (e.g., with petrolatum) . . .

negligible (adjective)

insignificant; very slight

The rim of the bell jar is sealed (e.g., with petrolatum) to ensure that loss of water by transpiration is **negligible**.

leakage (noun)

unwanted escape or emission of contents

The presence of organic solutes can be explained by **leakage** from cells that border on the xylem tissue.

said to be (expression)

    considered to be; judged to be

    Thus leaf cells may be **said to be** very effective but less than perfect demineralizers.

Vocabulary Exercises

A. Complete each numbered statement with a word or expression from the list.

leakage	driving force	persist
said to be	intact	viable
manifested	secures	yet to be determined
		seal

1. Industrial smoke emissions are the _____ behind the growth of the acid rain problem.

2. Retina reattachment surgery _____ the retina to the eye again.

3. Something that is transient does not _____ .

4. The etiology of essential hypertension is _____ .

5. A human baby born after seven months of gestation is often

    _____ .

6. A thing that is broken into little pieces is not _____ .

7. Hypertension can cause damage to the body before symptoms are

    _____ .

8. It is necessary to _____ bottles if you want their contents to remain sterile.

9. The NMR is _____ the most versatile of the new scanners.

10. We hope that _____ of radioactivity from nuclear power plants will not occur.

B. Choose a or b to complete each numbered statement.

1. Retinas are _____ reattached by laser surgery.
    a. dominantly
    b. readily

2. Hardiness is a _____ characteristic of successful food crops.
    a. dominant
    b. negligible

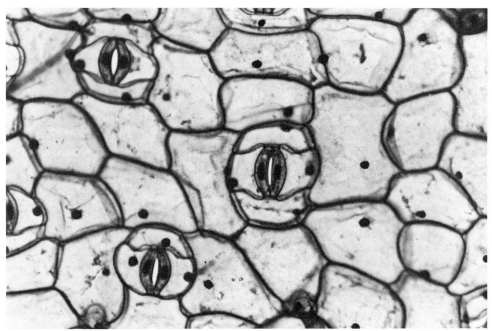

Microscopic view of trandescantia *leaf epidermis*
Carolina Biological Supply

3. Salinity is a _____ of sea water.
   a. driving force
   b. property

4. It is not known whether high blood pressure is _____ increased sodium intake.
   a. due to
   b. the driving force

5. Many plants _____ a substance called *sap*.
   a. secure
   b. exude

6. The print on this page does not extend all the way to the _____ .
   a. margins
   b. tips

7. The cargo aboard the space shuttle will be tied together in _____ .
   a. bundles
   b. margins

8. A drinking glass always has a _____ .
   a. tip
   b. rim

9. These two samples are almost the same; the differences between them are

_____ .
   a. dominant
   b. negligible

10. A good diet contains a great _____ of foods.
    a. leakage
    b. amplitude

11. The _____ of the nose is cartilaginous.
    a. tip
    b. rim

Comprehension

I. Meaning

EXERCISE

C. Respond T if the statement is true, F if the statement is false, or ? if the information cannot be determined from the reading on pages 43-45.

_____ 1. The selection describes the relationship between root pressure and guttation.

_____ 2. It is only recently that root pressure has been measured.

_____ 3. Bars are similar to pounds in that they are units of measurement.

_____ 4. Bars are units used in pressure measurements.

_____ 5. Root pressure is important to all plants.

_____ 6. Root pressure is dependent on guttation.

_____ 7. Guttation is a manifestation of root pressure.

_____ 8. When a plant is decapitated, the volume of xylem sap increases significantly over the amount normally lost in transpiration.

_____ 9. Inorganic solutes in guttation water come from the soil.

_____ 10. Hydathodes are typically parenchyma cells.

_____ 11. Diurnal refers to a 24-hour period.

_____ 12. Root pressures have a great amplitude.

_____ 13. It is difficult to demonstrate root pressure in the laboratory.

_____ 14. A stoma is a kind of pore.

_____ 15. Guttation water is exuded from leaves because the xylem elements end in a hydathode.

_____ 16. *Hydrostatic* is a word relating to water.

_____ 17. Remnants (¶ 11) are what remain of a substance after some process takes place.

_____ 18. Root pressure is demonstrated by placing a plant within a bell jar.

_____ 19. Diurnal rhythms are controlled by changes in temperature, light, and humidity.

_____ 20. Osmosis is related to transport.

II. *Reference*

EXERCISE

D. Choose a or b to indicate the reference for the italicized word or phrase in each statement taken from the reading on pages 43-45. Paragraph numbers are indicated.

    1. The *phenomenon* can be demonstrated readily in the laboratory. (¶ 1)
       a. root pressure
       b. xylem sap of roots

The stages of development of a bean plant, from seed to true leaf
Carolina Biological Supply

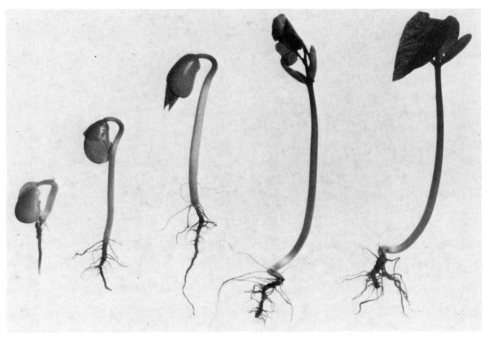

2. *This diurnal rhythm* persists even if a decapitated plant is placed in a growth chamber in which environmental conditions (e.g., temperature, light, humidity) are held constant. (¶ 4)
   a. fluctuation within a 24-hour period
   b. osmosis

3. Rhythms in biological processes (e.g., root pressure) are due to rhythms in protoplasmic activity—and *these* are reflected in changes in the properties of protoplasmic membranes. (¶ 4)
   a. rhythms in protoplasmic activity
   b. rhythms in biological processes

4. The volume of xylem sap exuded from the stump of a detopped viable root system is relatively small and only a fraction of the water that would be lost by the (intact) plant by transpiration during *the same period of time.* (¶ 5)
   a. the time that the xylem sap was exuded
   b. the time that the viable root system was detopped

5. If *it* has any role at all, it is only in very young plants, before leaves are developed and before transpiration becomes a dominant feature in the overall water economy of the plant. (¶ 6)
   a. root pressure
   b. life of most higher plants

6. If it has any role at all, *it* is only in very young plants, before leaves are developed and before transpiration becomes a dominant feature in the overall water economy of the plant. (¶ 6)
   a. root pressure
   b. impersonal *it*: no reference

7. As we saw earlier, transpiration accounts for the absorption of water by most species of higher plants during *their* adult lives. (¶ 6)
   a. of most species of higher plants
   b. the absorption of water

8. Typically a hydathode is an opening or pore in the leaf epidermis, around *which* are grouped several thin-walled parenchyma cells. (¶ 7)
   a. the hydathode
   b. the leaf epidermis

9. To demonstrate guttation in the laboratory, a potted, well-watered herbaceous plant, preferably *one* that is young and growing vigorously, is placed on a flat surface and covered with a bell jar. (¶ 9)
   a. potted, well-watered herbaceous plant
   b. laboratory

10. The inorganic solutes are mostly *those* absorbed by roots from the soil solution and carried passively to leaves in the upward-flowing xylem sap. (¶ 10)
    a. roots
    b. solutes

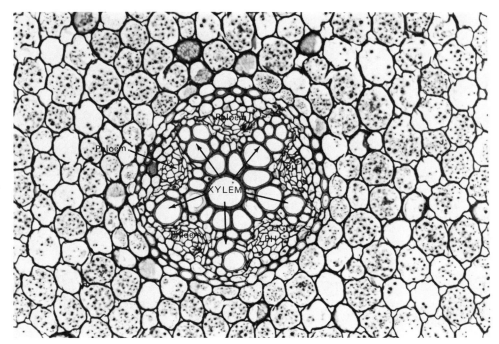

Cross-section of a stem, showing phloem and xylem
Carolina Biological Supply

11. This reduction in solute concentration is due to the fact that leaf cells absorb most of the dissolved salts passing through *their* xylem tissues. (¶ 11)
    a. of the solute concentration
    b. of the plant in which the leaf cells are found

12. The small amounts of inorganic solutes present in guttation water represent the remnants of dissolved salts not removed during *their* passage through leaves. (¶ 11)
    a. the remnants'
    b. the dissolved salts'

III. Syntax: Passive Voice

EXERCISE

E. Demonstrate your understanding of the passive voice by completing the following active voice paraphrases of sentences taken from the reading. The word you use can be taken unchanged from the original passive voice sentence.

1. We can demonstrate the _____ in the laboratory. (¶ 1)

2. Scientists attach a short piece of rubber tubing to a freshly decapitated young, well-watered herbaceous plant _____ . (¶ 1)

3. They then secure the _____ tube in a vertical position. (¶ 1)

4. _____ carried out the first demonstration and measurement of root pressure. (¶ 2)

5. We have _____ slightly higher values, although root pressures are usually in the +1- to +2-bar range. (¶ 2)

6. We have found that root _____ fluctuate. (¶ 4)

7. Even when we place a _____ plant in a growth chamber the diurnal rhythm persists. (¶ 4)

8. Even when we hold environmental conditions _____ the diurnal rhythm persists. (¶ 4)

9. _____ in the properties of protoplasmic membranes reflect rhythms in protoplasmic activities. (¶ 4)

10. We have not yet _____ the fundamental nature of biological rhythms. (¶ 4)

11. Scientists _____ regard root pressure of little importance in the life of most higher plants. (¶ 6)

12. Before the plant develops _____ , root pressure may be of importance. (¶ 6)

13. _____ is a visible manifestation of the development of root pressure. (¶ 6)

14. In guttation, groups of leaf cells exude _____ . (¶ 7)

15. There are groups of parenchyma cells around an _____ in the leaf epidermis. (¶ 7)

16. The presence of the hydathode forces xylem sap to _____ . (¶ 8)

17. The _____ exudes guttation water. (¶ 8)

18. Scientists place a young, vigorously growing _____ on a flat surface. (¶ 9)

19. They cover the _____ with a bell jar. (¶ 9)

20. Petrolatum seals the _____ of the jar. (¶ 9)

21. _____ from cells that border on the xylem tissue explains the presence of organic solutes. (¶ 10)

III. Syntax: Preposed Modifying Clusters

EXERCISE

F. Complete the following statements based on your understanding of the phrases with preposed modifying clusters taken from the reading. Choose your answers from the following list.

conduct	several
detopped	some time ago
experimental	thin walled
freshy decapitated	upward
herbaceous	viable
herbaceous	water
parenchyma	well watered
plants	well watered
pot	xylem
roots	xylem

1.-4. a freshly decapitated young, well-watered, herbaceous plant (¶ 1)

The plant is (1) _____ , (2) _____ ,

(3) _____ , and (4) _____ .

5.-7. an early experimental plant physiologist (¶ 2)

The physiologist specialized in (5) _____ .

He lived (6) _____ . His work was

(7) _____ .

8.-10. a detopped viable root system (¶ 5)

This system of (8) _____ is (9) _____

but still (10) _____ .

11.-13. several thin-walled parenchyma cells (¶ 7)

These cells are (11) _____ cells which are

(12) _____ . There are (13) _____

of them.

14.-16. water-conducting xylem elements (¶ 8)

These elements are (14) _____ elements. They

(15) _____ (16) _____ .

17.-19. a potted, well-watered, herbaceous plant (¶ 9)

this plant is a (17) _____ plant that is in a

(18) _____ and has been (19) _____ .

20.-21. upward-flowing xylem sap (¶ 10)

This sap is (20) _____ sap. It flows in an

(21) _____ direction.

The dieffenbachia, *or dumb cane, is a common household plant*

© John H. Gerard, National Audubon Society.

Prediction: Logic

Often your ability to predict what will follow a statement in a narrative will depend on simple logic. Logic is based on your experience and is a cognitive rather than a language skill.

examples: John does not like laboratory experiments.
(Logic tells us that some reasons why John does not like laboratory experiments will follow.)

The maglev is able to travel at great speeds very smoothly.
(Logic tells us that what will follow is an explanation of how this is possible.)

IV. Prediction: Logic

EXERCISE

G. Use logic to predict what will most probably come next. Choose the more likely response. The statements all come from the reading on pages 43–45. Paragraph numbers are indicated.

1. The phenomenon can be demonstrated readily in the laboratory. (¶ 1)
   a. how this can be demonstrated
   b. what can be demonstrated

2. Guttation water is exuded from groups of leaf cells called hydathodes. (¶ 7)
   a. something about leaf cells in general
   b. something about hydathodes

3. Guttation depends on root pressure. (¶ 8)
   a. the relation of guttation to root pressure
   b. where guttation takes place

4. To demonstrate guttation in the laboratory, a potted, well-watered, herbaceous plant, preferably one that is young and growing vigorously, is placed on a flat surface and covered with a bell jar. (¶ 9)
   a. more details about this procedure
   b. something about vigorous growth

5. Guttation water contains small amounts of both organic and inorganic solutes.
   a. something about the solutes
   b. an explanation of when guttation water does not contain small amounts of solutes

LESSON FOUR
Materials

Textbook Features

The front matter of a textbook is a helpful clue to how important this particular work may be to your needs. The use of the front matter need not be time-consuming or difficult, but it is a fundamental first step in materials selection and evaluation, and it serves as an introduction to the work.

Preface

All books have a title page and copyright page. Virtually all have a table of contents. Most have a preface written by the author. This feature is most helpful in informing the reader of the author's intention or purpose, in providing his or her rationale for organizing the material in a particular way, and in giving a general idea of the difficulty level or sophistication of the material. In addition, authors sometimes include a description of their research method. Acknowledgments and permissions for the use of published material are sometimes in the preface if they are not extensive and not included elsewhere in the book.

Preface

EXERCISE

A. The following excerpts come from the prefaces of two science textbooks. Read them and then select the correct lettered response to each numbered question.

> This book aims to present the basic knowledge of astronomy to readers having no training in mathematics or science beyond a modest secondary school level. Although knowledge in the physical sciences can be concisely expressed in mathematical form, most of it can be well transmitted and appreciated with little mathematical formulation. A lack of mathematical training or aptitude need turn no one from the profitable reading of this book. Nevertheless we expect that astronomy and physics students, as well as space scientists and engineers, and amateur astronomers, will also find in this *Survey of the Universe* a convenient introduction to more advanced texts.
>
> We present the reader with an overview of the rapidly expanding knowledge of the physical universe. We hope to impart some of the excitement and enthusiasm for astronomy that have drawn the three of us into lifetimes of research and teaching. The structure of this knowledge is neither rigid nor static but continually evolves and expands. Every statement, every conclusion, every generalization is suspect, subject to review, change and modification, as observation and theory mutually restructure and expand our understanding of the universe. Theories are fallible under the brutal scrutiny of new observing techniques and observations. Even observations are not sacrosanct, because they can be improved and reinterpreted. On the other hand, our continuously restructured body of knowledge represents a closer and closer approximation to the universe as we can observe it. Only the exciting frontiers of exploration are ill defined.
>
> Donald H. Menzel, Fred L. Whipple, and Gerard de Vaucouleurs,
Survey of the Universe (Englewood Cliffs, N.J.:
Prentice-Hall, Inc., 1970), p. v.

Physics for Scientists and Engineers is meant to be used for a two-semester or three-semester course in classical physics; either of these courses usually requires a one-chapter introduction to quantum physics. It is assumed that the student is studying calculus concurrently. Thus, in the beginning of the text we assume little knowledge of calculus and introduce in detail the mathematical concepts we need, but as the book progresses we assume more and more familiarity with calculus.

THE UNITY OF PHYSICS   In our experience, some students are overwhelmed by physics because they treat each topic as if it were a separate subject. To try to overcome this tendency, we point out the interrelationships that emphasize the unity of physics. By noting the common starting point for many topics, the parallel developments of some topics, and the recurring use of the same mathematical techniques, we hope that the student will recognize and use the fact that the large variety of topics covered are developed from a relatively few basic concepts using only a few different mathematical methods. We note these interrelationships as they occur in the main body of the text, in chapter introductions and summaries, and in overview sections that come between some chapters, as appropriate.

FLEXIBILITY   We have organized the book to allow flexibility in its use. This flexibility has been achieved by (1) identifying in the text certain sections and sub-sections that can be omitted without affecting the use of the rest of the book, (2) writing the text so that certain chapters can be omitted in their entirety, (3) including brief introductions to certain topics at an early stage so that the more detailed discussions or applications that follow in later chapters can be omitted if desired, and (4) writing the text so that certain topics can be covered out of sequence at the instructor's discretion. We will give examples of each of these below. Because of this flexibility, the book can be used for both two- and three-semester courses and with some variations in topic sequence.

Shelden H. Radin and Robert T. Folk, *Physics for Scientists and Engineers* (Englewood Cliffs, N.J.: Prentice-Hall, Inc., 1982), p. xiii.

1. Which book would be likely to be more difficult for the average reader?
   a. the first one
   b. the second one
   c. It is impossible to guess.
   d. neither

2. What formal academic background is probably necessary in order to use *Physics for Scientists and Engineers*?
   a. a thorough knowledge of calculus
   b. a two-semester or three-semester course in classical physics
   c. university-level mathematics
   d. a strong academic background at the secondary-school level and a serious interest in science

3. Which book will rely more on the interrelationship between its subject matter and mathematics?
   a. *Physics for Scientists and Engineers*
   b. *Survey of the Universe*
   c. Neither book will use math to any extent.
   d. Both books will use math about equally.

4. Which book probably presents a more formal, in-depth coverage of its subject matter?
   a. *Physics for Scientists and Engineers*
   b. *Survey of the Universe*
   c. Neither book appears to present an in-depth approach to its subject.
   d. Both books probably present an equally in-depth coverage of their subject matter.

5. What did the excerpts from the prefaces not include?
   a. a specific listing of the contents
   b. a general description of the authors' point of view
   c. the suggestion that although the subject matter is regarded as difficult, the authors have tried to simplify it
   d. a discussion about the student using the text

Introduction

Another item that appears at the beginning of many books is an introduction. This sometimes appears as part of the text itself, paginated in arabic numbers, although it is frequently included in the roman-numeral pagination of the front matter.

An introduction is similar to a preface in that they both serve as openers to a text. However, an introduction is usually part of the subject matter of the text itself, rather than an explanation of the author's intention or the book's scope. It is therefore essential to read the introduction when you are actually using a book. A preface, on the other hand, is more useful in helping you to decide whether or not to use a book in the first place.

example:

Endocrinology is a subdiscipline of the broader field, physiology, and is concerned with chemical messengers or *hormones*, substances secreted by cells of endocrine glands (ductless glands) and tissues that regulate the activity of other cells in the body.

Mac E. Hadley, *Endocrinology* (Englewood Cliffs, N.J.: Prentice-Hall, Inc., 1984), p. 1.

Introduction

EXERCISE

B. Read the following excerpts. Then mark each one P if you think it comes from a preface or I if you think it comes from an introduction.

1. Although the fungi are a diverse group of organisms, a feature which they have in common with each other is their mode of nutrition.[1]

2. Development of a multicellular organism commences upon fertilization and subsequent division of the egg.[2]

3. Since the material covered in some entire chapters is somewhat specialized or is clearly not necessary for the development of other basic concepts, these chapters can be omitted at the discretion of the instructor.[3]

4. We would like to express our appreciation to our colleagues for their support and advice throughout the development of the text and while using the Lehigh version in their classes.[4]

5. Because scientific knowledge is the handiwork of individual human beings and consists only of what they have individually contributed, we attempt to show how the major contributors have developed the structure historically.[5]

Lists of Illustrations and Lists of Data Tables

Illustration lists and lists of data tables are often included in the front matter when the book has only a few important illustrations or data tables and these are thought to be of value to many readers. In the case of illustrations, if there are several different kinds, the list may be subdivided by type of illustration, such as charts, maps, plates, or figures.

Many books, particularly those with extensive illustrative matter tightly tied to the text, do not include a list of illustrations at the beginning of the book. When a list is included, however, it also gives the page numbers.

Occasionally, when an insert of color photographs or illustrations occurs, the entire insert is unpaginated and will carry the notation, "facing page . . . " or "following page . . . ."

The illustration list is helpful when you are using a text for reference only and do

---

[1] Elizabeth Moore-Landecker, *Fundamentals of the Fungi*, 2nd ed. (Englewood Cliffs, N.J.: Prentice-Hall, Inc., 1982), p. 3.

[2] Mac E. Hadley, *Endocrinology* (Englewood Cliffs, N.J.: Prentice-Hall, Inc., 1984), p. 1.

[3] Shelden H. Radin and Robert T. Folk, *Physics for Scientists and Engineers* (Englewood Cliffs, N.J.: Prentice-Hall, Inc., 1982), p. xiv.

[4] *Ibid*, p. xv.

[5] Donald H. Menzel, Fred L. Whipple, and Gerard de Vaucouleurs, *Survey of the Universe* (Englewood Cliffs, N.J.: Prentice-Hall, Inc., 1970), p. v.

not intend to use it in its entirety. It is sometimes said that a picture is worth a thousand words, and if this is true, a good illustration list can save you a lot of time reading.

More common in scientific and technical books is a list of tables. When such a list occurs, it follows the table of contents and the illustration list. Authors and editors include a data table listing to help two types of readers: the person who is using the text on a daily basis and will want to glance often at tables of data that are frequently referred to in the text, and the person who is merely consulting this particular book because of its data tables. Examples of data tables would be a geological time chart in a paleontology textbook, a periodic table of the elements in a basic chemistry textbook, and a list of coefficients of drag in an aerodynamics text.

Lists of Illustrations and Lists of Data Tables

EXERCISE

C. Respond T if the statement is true, or F if the statement is false.

_____ 1. If a book has no illustration list, we know it is unillustrated.

_____ 2. Maps are included in illustration lists rather than in data-table lists.

_____ 3. Data-table lists generally precede the table of contents.

_____ 4. Illustration lists are found in the front matter.

_____ 5. It is essential to consult all illustrations before beginning to use a text.

_____ 6. An illustration list can save you time reading the text and searching for illustrations.

_____ 7. Data-table lists and illustration lists are of value only to the reference reader, not to the everyday text user.

"To the Teacher" and "To the Student"

Front matter sometimes includes a section entitled "To the Teacher" or "To the Student" or some variant of that idea. This section, although not necessarily essential to your use of the text, can be one of the most important elements in the book, particularly for a text used in a classroom.

In this section the author suggests to the teacher or the student the ways in which the text can be most beneficially used. Many instructors follow this advice, at least partially. Knowing what the instructor is planning to do with the text will give you a good idea of what his or her expectations of you will be.

"To the Teacher" and "To the Student"

EXERCISE

D. Read the following excerpts from a popular grammar text. Then choose a or b to answer each numbered question.

> 3. Some of the exercises are designated ORAL (BOOKS CLOSED). It is important that the students not look at their texts during these exercises, no matter how much they might want to. Even intermediate students should soon learn to concentrate on what you are saying and respond quickly. ("Mind-writing" should be discouraged; instead the students should be encouraged to open their mouths and see what happens. A mistake is not of earthshaking importance.) Be flexible in the responses you accept. The main criterion is whether or not the student has understood what you said and is producing the target structure competently and communicatively. Minor changes in wording are not important. Use the ORAL (BOOKS CLOSED) exercises freely. In many of these exercises, the entries are not intended to be "read as is," but rather are intended to prompt your mind as you engage your students (individually, not chorally) in short exchanges. Put entries into particular contexts where possible, as though you were initiating a conversation; pursue interesting responses, grammar aside; add entries that are directly relevant to your class and the here-and-now classroom context; delete irrelevant entries; encourage the students to use the exercises for out-of-class practice; use part of an exercise one day and part another day if you wish; return to the exercises from previously covered chapters for quick reviews at the beginning of a class period.
>
> The symbol (. . .) indicates that you are to supply the name of a class member. Place and time expressions are often in parentheses, indicating that you are to supply an expression relevant to the people in your class.
>
> The exercises designated ORAL are to be done with books open but require no writing and no preparation.

Betty S. Azar, *Understanding and Using English Grammar* (Englewood Cliffs, N.J.: Prentice-Hall, Inc., 1981), pp. xiv-xv.

1. How will oral exercises be presented?
   a. some with books open and others with books closed
   b. with "mind writing"
2. How will mistakes be handled?
   a. with a flexible response
   b. with a degree of permissiveness
3. How does the author feel about various answers to the same question?
   a. She believes there is only one "right" answer to each question.
   b. She believes any reasonable answer should be acceptable to the instructor.
4. What is the goal of the oral exercises?
   a. free communication using the target structures
   b. memorization of target structures and unchanged wording

5. In what form should these exercises be taught?
   a. in any form that suits the teacher and his or her personal goals
   b. completely, from start to finish in one class period

6. What does enclosure in parentheses indicate?
   a. that the teacher should make changes relevant to his or her classroom situation
   b. that the material is optional

7. What preparation by students is necessary for the oral exercises?
   a. writing
   b. none

Reading and Interpreting Charts, Tables, Diagrams, Graphs, Line Drawings, and Schematic Illustrations

Diagrams

Diagrams, graphs, line drawings, and schematic illustrations are all visual, symbolic presentations of ideas, information, and other data. It is not always easy to label these, as the distinction between some line drawings and schematic illustrations is not great. What is important, however, is being able to derive information from these features.

The simplest kind of diagram is the block diagram. This type is most common in technical writing, particularly when the author wants to show a sequence of occurrences or steps in a process, or how one factor influences another. Arrows are often used to connect the blocks and to show the order in which they should be read, thus symbolizing the order in which the process occurs.

example:

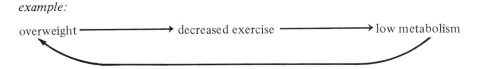

overweight ⟶ decreased exercise ⟶ low metabolism

In this diagram the author has pictured or symbolized the "vicious circle" of how overweight is perpetuated. The arrows can be read as standing for the phrase "leads to."

Other diagrams of this type can become very complex, showing the order in which multiple occurrences took place and the combination of numerous factors affecting the outcome of a situation. A chemical reaction is one example of such a diagram.

$$^-O - P - O - CH_2 - C - COOH$$

with the structure showing:
$$\begin{array}{ccc} & O & \quad\quad O \\ & \parallel & \quad\quad \parallel \\ ^-O - & P - O - CH_2 - & C - COOH \\ & \mid & \\ & O^- & \end{array}$$

Diagrams

EXERCISE

E. Look at the following diagrams and choose the correct lettered responses to answer the questions about them.

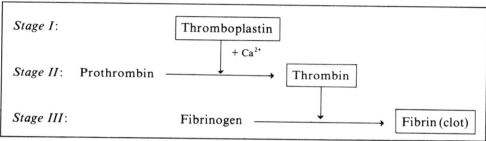

From William S. Hoar, *General and Comparative Physiology* (Englewood Cliffs, N.J.: Prentice-Hall, Inc., 1983), p. 463.

1. Where does this process begin?
   a. with thromboplastin
   b. with a clot
2. What is the end result of this process?
   a. fibrin
   b. fibrinogen
3. What gives rise to thrombin?
   a. prothrombin and another factor
   b. prothrombin alone
4. How is fibrinogen converted to fibrin?
   a. through the action of thrombin
   b. in three stages

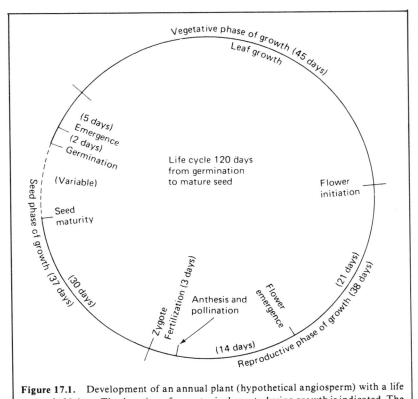

Figure 17.1. Development of an annual plant (hypothetical angiosperm) with a life cycle of 120 days. The duration of some typical events during growth is indicated. The block in germination, whether due to deficiency of moisture or to some dormancy factor, is of variable duration.

From G. Ray Noggle and George J. Fritz, *Introductory Plant Physiology*, 2nd ed. (Englewood Cliffs, N.J.: Prentice-Hall, Inc., 1983), p. 517.

5. What is this diagram about?
   a. the life cycle of a plant
   b. how to care for plants

6. How should this diagram be read?
   a. clockwise
   b. counterclockwise

7. What are the three phases in the development of the organism described?
   a. germination, flower initiation, and pollination
   b. the seed phase, the vegetative phase, and the reproductive phase

8. What occurs in the life cycle after the plant has reached maturity?
   a. The mature plant produces seeds and the cycle continues.
   b. The cycle ends.

9. How long does it take for the flowers to emerge?
   a. 21 days
   b. 38 days

10. In which phase do the leaves grow?
    a. the reproductive phase
    b. the vegetative phase

11. How long does it take for the seed to germinate?
    a. The period varies.
    b. 120 days

12. Why did the author choose a circle for this diagram?
    a. to symbolize an unending sequence, as a circle has no beginning and no end
    b. because a seed is round

13. What is the diagram on page 71 about?
    a. places
    b. time

14. What are the main eras?
    a. Quaternary and Tertiary
    b. Cenozoic, Mesozoic, Paleozoic, and Precambrian

15. Which era is the most recent?
    a. Cenozoic
    b. Precambrian

16. Which period lasted longer?
    a. Permian
    b. Ordovician

17. How long have we been in the Holocene?
    a. more than 10,000 years
    b. since the beginning of the Cenozoic

18. What are the eras directly subdivided into?
    a. periods
    b. epochs

19. When did the Devonian period take place?
    a. between 360 and 395 million years ago
    b. between 35 and 40 million years ago

20. How long did the Triassic last?
    a. 30 to 35 million years
    b. 195 to 225 million years

21. Why is this material presented in a vertical format?
    a. because it fits well on a rectangular page
    b. because it symbolizes or represents the way the earth's layers are laid down, with the older layers below the newer

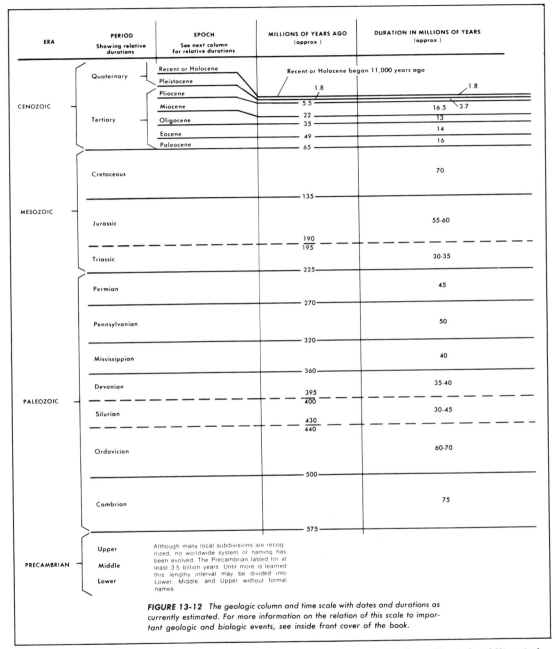

ERA	PERIOD Showing relative durations	EPOCH See next column for relative durations	MILLIONS OF YEARS AGO (approx.)	DURATION IN MILLIONS OF YEARS (approx.)
CENOZOIC	Quaternary	Recent or Holocene	Recent or Holocene began 11,000 years ago	
		Pleistocene		
		Pliocene	1.8	1.8
	Tertiary	Miocene	5.5	16.5 3.7
		Oligocene	22	13
		Eocene	35	14
		Paleocene	49	16
			65	
MESOZOIC	Cretaceous			70
			135	
	Jurassic			55-60
			190	
			195	
	Triassic			30-35
			225	
PALEOZOIC	Permian			45
			270	
	Pennsylvanian			50
			320	
	Mississippian			40
			360	
	Devonian			35-40
			395	
			400	
	Silurian			30-45
			430	
			440	
	Ordovician			60-70
			500	
	Cambrian			75
			575	
PRECAMBRIAN	Upper	Although many local subdivisions are recognized, no worldwide system of naming has been evolved. The Precambrian lasted for at least 3.5 billion years. Until more is learned this lengthy interval may be divided into Lower, Middle, and Upper without formal names.		
	Middle			
	Lower			

FIGURE 13-12 The geologic column and time scale with dates and durations as currently estimated. For more information on the relation of this scale to important geologic and biologic events, see inside front cover of the book.

From William Lee Stokes, Sheldon Judson, and M. Dane Picard, *Introduction to Geology: Physical and Historical* (Englewood Cliffs, N.J.: Prentice-Hall, Inc., 1978), p. 326.

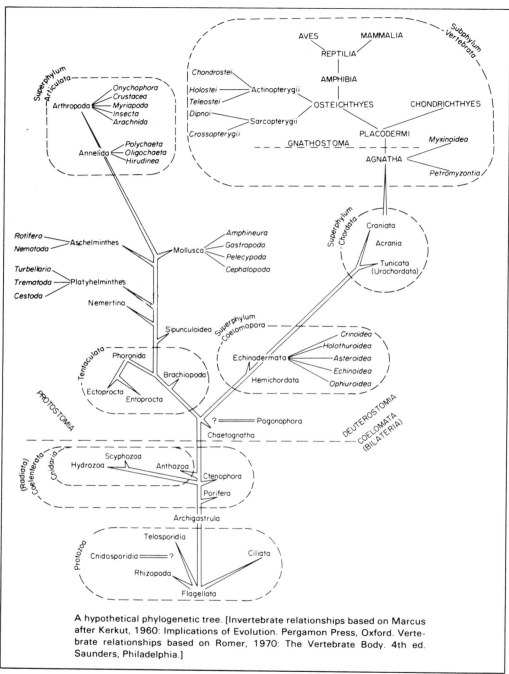

A hypothetical phylogenetic tree. [Invertebrate relationships based on Marcus after Kerkut, 1960: Implications of Evolution. Pergamon Press, Oxford. Vertebrate relationships based on Romer, 1970: The Vertebrate Body. 4th ed. Saunders, Philadelphia.]

From William S. Hoar, *General and Comparative Physiology* (Englewood Cliffs, N.J.: Prentice-Hall, Inc., 1983).

22. What is the diagram on page 72 about?
    a. the evolution of the animal kingdom
    b. a chemical chain reaction

23. What do Ciliata develop from?
    a. Flagellata
    b. Rhizopoda

24. What group of organisms did Cephalopoda give rise to?
    a. Mollusca
    b. none

25. What are two categories of Aschelminthes?
    a. Platyhelminthes and Nemertina
    b. Rotifera and Nematoda

26. Which group is evolutionarily more advanced?
    a. Reptilia
    b. Amphibia

27. Which is more directly related to Aves?
    a. Echinodermata
    b. Arthropoda

28. Why is this material presented in the form of a tree?
    a. because like a tree the animal kingdom developed into different branches from
       common roots
    b. to show that the animal and the plant kingdoms are very similar

Widespread Effects
of Air Pollution

Trees burned off by acid rain in Cubalāo, Brazil

In the past, as described above, air pollution was generally considered
basically an urban phenomenon. Consequently, the reasoning followed (and still persists among many people) that if urban pollutants could be diluted into the atmosphere at large, the final concentrations would be so low that they would cause no problems. This is
the old **assumption** that "dilution is the solution to pollution."
Therefore, taller smokestacks—up to 300 meters (1000 feet)—were
constructed for many industries and power plants in order to disperse 1
pollutants more widely. Also, power plants have been constructed
near coal fields in remote areas to remove their polluting effects
from the concentrated areas of cities and instead to disperse them in
areas of low pollution. However, much evidence **has accumulated**
that this practice simply results in spreading harmful effects more

From Bernard J. Nebel, *Environmental Science: The Way the World Works*
(Englewood Cliffs, N.J.: Prentice-Hall, Inc., 1981), pp. 328–331.

Acid rain damage to the nose and chin of a statue outside the Field Museum of Natural History in Chicago, Illinois, U.S.A.
AP/Wide World Photos

widely. This is illustrated by sulfur dioxides leading to the formation of acid rain and the widespread effect of air pollution on plants.

Sulfur Dioxide and Acid Rain

Sulfur dioxide (SO_2) is a gas that is poisonous to both plants and animals. Sulfur dioxide is produced mostly by power plants which burn coal to generate electricity. A large power plant may burn 10,000 tons of coal a day; if this coal is contaminated with 3 percent sulfur, some 900 tons of sulfur dioxide per day will be discharged.

As was noted earlier, in the natural cycle sulfur dioxide may be removed from the air through assimilation by soil microorganisms. However, to avoid the toxic effects in the meantime, industries have

2

attempted to dilute the sulfur dioxide by building taller smokestacks to disperse the gas. Ironically, this effort **has** largely **circumvented** the natural process of **assimilation** and created a new pollution problem. For the natural process to work, sulfur dioxide must come in contact with the soil and its microorganisms. Tall smokestacks **erected** to promote dilution largely prevent this. But everything must go somewhere eventually. Airborne for long periods, sulfur dioxide gradually reacts with oxygen and water **vapor** in the air to form sulfuric acid (H_2SO_4). Thus 900 tons of sulfur dioxide from one day's operation of a single large power plant become **some** 1500 tons of sulfuric acid by the addition of oxygen and hydrogen to the molecule. The sulfuric acid is diluted by rainfall but even then the rain is commonly 10 to 100 times more acid than normal; in some cases it is even 1000 times more acid than normal. Nitrogen oxides **contribute** in a similar way by forming nitric acid (HNO_3). Rainwater containing such acids is called *acid rain*. 3

The effects of acid rain are numerous. Perhaps most **striking** is the **dissolving** of limestone and marble. Many statues and monuments **have been eroded** more in the last 50 years than they had been in the previous 200. It also increases the corrosion rate of all metal structures, such as bridges. However, the most insidious long-term effect of acid rain is a gradual lowering of the pH of water and soil. This can lead to **gross** alteration of aquatic ecosystems and a greatly increased rate of leaching. For example, Cornell University biologist Carl Schofield has observed that more than half the lakes in the Adirondack Mountains (northern New York State) above 600 meters (1800 feet) have become highly acidic and 90 percent of these are **devoid** of fish. The death of the fish is due to both the acidity and the leaching effect of acid rain. In addition to decreasing pH, the acid **precipitation** leaches from the soil aluminum compounds which are toxic to fish. In another study, the water **draining** from a forest area in New Hampshire was monitored; it was found that leaching of nutrients had increased three- to tenfold because of acid rain. This constitutes a serious loss of fertility, which ultimately **must be reflected** in a decline in productivity. 4

Diabolically, the effects of acid rain are observed in what are generally considered unpolluted areas, hundreds of miles from pollution sources. The emissions which cause acid rain in the Adirondacks come from industries along the Great Lakes. The acid rain in New Hampshire comes from New York City. Similarly, sulfur dioxide originating in England has caused extensive acid rain damage to lake and stream ecosystems in Sweden. Almost everywhere that the pH of rainwater is measured, observers note some increase in acidity over that of pure rainwater. Therefore lesser effects **can be presumed** to extend even more widely. A United Nations conference in the fall of 1977 recognized acid rain as a global pollution problem. 5

Cornell: university in New York State

New Hampshire: state in northeastern U.S.

Great Lakes: lakes in north central U.S.

Federal air pollution laws **restrict** the sulfur dioxide emissions somewhat, but to prevent the impact of acid rain, regulations need to be much more **stringent**. Unfortunately, because of shortages of high-quality (low-sulfur) oil and natural gas, some leaders in industry and government are asking that air pollution regulations be relaxed to allow the burning of more coal and low-grade oil, which have high sulfur contents. If this occurs, acid rain problems can only become more severe. Obviously dilution is not the solution to pollution in the case of sulfur dioxide.

6

Air Pollution and Plant Growth

There have been **countless** cases of vegetation—agricultural crops, ornamental plants, and forest species—being severely damaged or killed by air pollution. However, even more insidious than the outright visible damage, air pollution is also responsible for a general reduction in plant growth which can occur without other **conspicuous** signs of damage or abnormality. For example a recent study in Yonkers, New York, showed that photochemical smog reduced sweet corn and alfalfa yields by 15 percent. Field experiments at Riverside, California, showed that yields of sweet corn were reduced by 72 percent, alfalfa 38 percent, radishes 38 percent, grapes 60 percent, navel oranges 50 percent, and lemons 30 percent as compared to similar plants grown in clean, filtered air. Another study in the San Bernardino Mountains of California showed that timber production had been reduced by 75 percent. Many other studies show similar results. Air pollution has forced the complete abandonment of citrus growing in certain areas of California and vegetable growing in certain areas of New Jersey—areas that were formerly among the most productive in the country.

7

The effects in most areas of the country are not this severe, for many important agricultural areas receive relatively little pollution, but nationwide the average loss of agricultural and forest production is estimated to be between 1 and 2 percent. This apparently small percentage is far from insignificant. With an annual corn production in the United States of about 6 million bushels, a 2-percent loss amounts to about 120 million bushels.

8

Yonkers: town near New York City

Vocabulary

assumption (noun)

belief; supposition

This is the old **assumption** that "dilution is the solution to pollution."

to accumulate (verb)

> to collect; to increase

> However, much evidence **has accumulated** that this practice simply results in spreading harmful effects more widely.

to circumvent (verb)

> to help to overcome; to help to avoid

> Ironically, this effort **has** largely **circumvented** the natural process of assimilation and created a new pollution problem.

assimilation (noun)

> incorporation of one thing into another; absorption to the point of integration

> Ironically, this effort has largely circumvented the natural process of **assimilation** and created a new pollution problem.

to erect (verb)

> to build; to construct, especially a long, tall structure; to raise

> Tall smokestacks **erected** to promote dilution largely prevent this.

erecting a statue

some (adverb)

> About; approximately

> Thus 900 tons of sulfur dioxide from one day's operation of a single large power plant become **some** 1500 tons of sulfuric acid by the addition of oxygen and hydrogen to the molecule.

vapor (noun)

> steam or mist suspended in the air

Airborne for long periods, sulfur dioxide gradually reacts with oxygen and water **vapor** in the air to form sulfuric acid (H_2SO_4).

to contribute (verb)

> to supply along with other suppliers

Nitrogen oxides **contribute** in a similar way by forming nitric acid (HNO_3).

striking (adjective)

> prominent; important; impressive

Perhaps most **striking** is the dissolving of limestone and marble.

to dissolve (verb)

> to disintegrate; to pass into component parts, solution, or liquid form

Perhaps most striking is the **dissolving** of limestone and marble.

to erode (verb)

> to wear away; to corrode

Many statues and monuments **have been eroded** more in the last 50 years than they had been in the previous 200.

gross (adjective)

large; large-scale

This can lead to **gross** alteration of aquatic ecosystems and a greatly increased rate of leaching.

devoid [of] (adjective)

completely lacking

Cornell University biologist Carl Schofield has observed that more than half the lakes in the Adirondack Mountains (northern New York State) above 600 meters (1800 feet) have become highly acidic and 90 percent of these are **devoid of** fish.

trees devoid of leaves

precipitation (noun)

any form of rain or snow

In addition to decreasing pH, the acid **precipitation** leaches from the soil aluminum compounds which are toxic to fish.

Rain is a form of precipitation.

to drain (verb)

> to empty; to cause water to go out from

> In another study, the water **draining** from a forest area in New Hampshire was monitored.

to reflect (verb)

> to show; to demonstrate

> This constitutes a serious loss of fertility, which ultimately **must be reflected** in a decline in productivity.

to presume (verb)

> to suppose; to imagine

> Therefore, lesser effects **can be presumed** to extend even more widely.

to restrict (verb)

> to keep within certain limits; to prevent from growing

> Federal air pollution laws **restrict** the sulfur dioxide emissions somewhat, but to prevent the impact of acid rain, regulations need to be much more stringent.

stringent (adjective)

> strict; restrictive; severe

> Federal air pollution laws restrict the sulfur dioxide emissions somewhat, but to prevent the impact of acid rain, regulations need to be much more **stringent**.

countless (adjective)

> numerous; more than may be counted; an unknown, but large, number of

> There have been **countless** cases of vegetation—agricultural crops, ornamental plants, and forest species—being severely damaged or killed by air pollution.

conspicuous (adjective)

> obvious; very noticeable

> However, even more insidious than the outright visible damage, air pollution is also responsible for a general reduction in plant growth which can occur without other **conspicuous** signs of damage or abnormality.

Vocabulary Exercises

A. Complete the following statements with words from the list.

erode   contribute   striking
drain   devoid   some
vapor   circumvent

1. _____ 500 people enrolled in the course.

2. A boiling pot releases water _____ into the air.

3. It is difficult to _____ the process of acid rain formation once contaminants are released into the atmosphere.

4. Both the buildup of stress along fault lines and underground rock movements _____ to earthquake probability.

5. Rainfall in mountainous areas can _____ large zones in a short time.

6. A _____ example of animal ferocity is the great white shark.

7. When special scrubbers are installed in industrial smokestacks, it is hoped that emissions will be _____ of harmful contaminants.

8. Rivers _____ water from the land and from precipitation in the air.

B. Choose a or b to complete each numbered statement.

1. Increased radon levels in ground water _____ subterranean seismic activity.
   a. reflect
   b. circumvent

2. _____ of the nutrients in food is what constitutes eating.
   a. Assumption
   b. Assimilation

3. Many statues have been _____ in honor of Galileo.
   a. accumulated
   b. erected

4. Sugar _____ in water.
   a. drains
   b. dissolves

5. _____ can be extremely acidic.
   a. Precipitation
   b. Assumption

6. Clinicians _____ that a link exists between salt consumption and hypertension.
   a. restrict
   b. presume

7. _____ disturbances of vision may result from the use of some drugs.
   a. Gross
   b. Stringent

8. A _____ lack of animals in an environment that previously had them suggests the existence of a noxious agent.
   a. conspicuous
   b. countless

A source of sulfur emissions: the industrial smokestack

A.T.&T. Co. Photo Center

9. Evidence has _____ that plants such as amaranth may contribute to solving the problem of hunger in areas of marginal fertility.
   a. accumulated
   b. circumvented

10. _____ tremors have occurred in the area of California's San Andreas fault.
    a. Countless
    b. Stringent

11. It will be necessary in the future to at least partially _____ industrial sulfur emissions.
    a. erect
    b. restrict

12. _____ measures are difficult to implement, but when they are necessary they must be adopted.
    a. Conspicuous
    b. Stringent

13. The old _____ that earthquakes cannot be prevented is beginning to be questioned.
    a. assimilation
    b. assumption

Comprehension

I. Meaning

EXERCISE

C. Choose a or b to answer each numbered question. Refer to the reading on pages 74-77 as necessary.

1. What was the assumption about air pollution in the past?
   a. It would persist among many people.
   b. It was really a problem of the cities.

2. Because of this, what idea followed?
   a. If contaminants were widely dispersed, they would be essentially harmless.
   b. The pollution solution is concentration.

3. Why were taller smokestacks constructed?
   a. as a solution to the pollution problem
   b. to concentrate pollutants more accurately

4. What does *diluted* mean?
   a. made more concentrated
   b. made less concentrated

5. In paragraph 1, what is the meaning of *solution*?
   a. a liquid containing a dissolved substance
   b. a remedy

6. What is now known about purposeful wide dispersal of contaminants?
   a. It contributes to acid rain formation.
   b. It helps overcome the acid rain problem.

7. What is the major source of sulfur dioxide?
   a. coal-generating electricity-burning plants
   b. coal-burning electricity-generating plants

8. What is implied about coal in general?
   a. It is naturally contaminated with sulfur.
   b. It contaminates sulfur naturally.

9. What removes a certain percentage of sulfur dioxide already in the air?
   a. microscopic plants and animals found in soil
   b. scrubbers

10. Why have the tall smokestacks made it impossible for the natural assimilation of airborne contaminants to take place?
    a. because the contaminants don't come into contact with the ground
    b. because everything must go somewhere eventually

11. What is ironic about the attempt to lessen the impact of airborne pollutants by building tall smokestacks?
    a. Building these has had the paradoxical effect of worsening the problem.
    b. Building these has had the desired effect that they were built for.

12. What conclusion can you draw about sulfuric acid formation?
    a. It occurs immediately from the reaction of sulfur dioxide with the oxygen and water vapor in the air.
    b. It is a gradual process made possible by the length of the acid's airborne period.

13. How acidic can acid rain be?
    a. 1000 times more acidic than normal rainfall
    b. more than the last 50 years

14. What are some of the most impressive effects of acid rain?
    a. the erosion, corrosion, and dissolving of metal, marble, and stone
    b. the immediate lowering of soil and water pH

15. What does the word *insidious* suggest?
    a. gradual, bad, and not quite visible
    b. gross, sudden, and obvious

16. What substances other than acids harm aquatic wildlife?
    a. aluminum compounds
    b. precipitation leaches

17. What other eventual effect does acid rain have?
    a. the draining of forest water
    b. a reduction in agricultural output due to nutrient leaching

Acid rain damage to trees near Bonn, West Germany
AP/Wide World Photos

18. How far from pollution sources can the effects of acid rain be observed?
    a. in the Adirondacks
    b. hundreds of miles away

19. What conclusion can be drawn about the widespread effects of acid rain?
    a. The lesser effects probably extend very widely.
    b. The widespread effects are more than that of pure rainwater.

20. What does *relaxed* mean in paragraph 6?
    a. less stringent
    b. more stringent

21. What does *outright* mean in paragraph 7?
    a. insidious
    b. obvious

II. Reference

D. Choose a or b to indicate the reference for the italicized word or phrase in each statement taken from the reading on pages 74-77. Paragraph numbers are indicated.

1. *This* is the old assumption that "dilution is the solution to pollution." (¶ 1)
   a. final concentrations of pollutants
   b. the reasoning

2. Also, power plants have been constructed near coal fields in remote areas to remove *their* polluting effects from the concentrated areas of cities and instead to disperse them in areas of low pollution. (¶ 1)
   a. coal fields'
   b. power plants'

3. Also, power plants have been constructed near coal fields in remote areas to remove their polluting effects from the concentrated areas of cities and instead to disperse *them* in areas of low pollution. (¶ 1)
   a. power plants
   b. polluting effects

4. However, much evidence has accumulated that *this practice* simply results in spreading harmful effects more widely. (¶ 1)
   a. putting power plants near coal fields in remote areas
   b. constructing power plants right in the cities

5. *This* is illustrated by sulfur dioxides leading to the formation of acid rain and the widespread effect of air pollution on plants. (¶ 1)
   a. formation of acid rain
   b. spreading of harmful effects more widely

6. A large power plant may burn 10,000 tons of coal a day; if *this coal* is contaminated with 3 percent sulfur, some 900 tons of sulfur dioxide per day will be discharged. (¶ 2)
   a. the 10,000 tons burned by the large power plant
   b. a specific type of coal

7. Ironically, *this effort* has largely circumvented the natural process of assimilation and created a new pollution problem. (¶ 3)
   a. avoiding the toxic effects
   b. building taller smokestacks

8. For *the natural process* to work, sulfur dioxide must come in contact with the soil and its microorganisms. (¶ 3)
   a. the assimilation of toxins
   b. the assimilation of microorganisms

9. Tall smokestacks erected to promote dilution largely prevent *this*. (¶ 3)
   a. the natural process
   b. dilution

10. The sulfuric acid is diluted by rainfall but even then the rain is commonly 10 to 100 times more acid than normal; in some cases *it* is even 1000 times more acid than normal. (¶ 3)
   a. the acid
   b. the rain

11. Rainwater containing *such acids* is called acid rain. (¶ 3)
   a. H_2SO_4 and HNO_3
   b. those acids 10 to 100 times stronger

12. Many statues and monuments have been eroded more in the last 50 years than *they* had been in the previous 200. (¶ 4)
   a. the last 50 years
   b. statues and monuments

13. *It* also increases the corrosion rate of all metal structures, such as bridges. (¶ 4)
   a. impersonal *it*; no reference
   b. acid rain

14. *This* can lead to gross alteration of aquatic ecosystems and a greatly increased rate of leaching. (¶ 4)
   a. the gradual lowering of the pH of water and soil
   b. the corrosion of all metal structures

15. Cornell University biologist Carl Schofield has observed that more than half the lakes in the Adirondack Mountains (northern New York State) above 600 meters (1800 feet) have become highly acidic and 90 percent of *these* are devoid of fish. (¶ 4)
   a. the lakes
   b. the Adirondacks

16. In another study, the water draining from a forest area in New Hampshire was monitored; *it* was found that leaching of nutrients had increased three- to tenfold because of acid rain. (¶ 4)
   a. impersonal *it*; no reference
   b. the forest

17. *This* constitutes a serious loss of fertility, which ultimately will be reflected in a decline in productivity. (¶ 4)
   a. increased leaching of nutrients
   b. water draining from the land

18. Almost everywhere that the pH of rainwater is measured, observers note some increase in acidity over *that* of pure rainwater. (¶ 5)
   a. the acidity
   b. the increase

19. If *this* occurs, acid rain problems can only become more severe. (¶ 6)
   a. relaxing pollution regulations
   b. shortages of high-quality oil and natural gas

Extreme acid rain damage to marble west-facing balustrade
NPS/USGS Photo by D. Dwornik

III. Syntax: Tenses of the Passive Voice

EXERCISE

E. Read the following sentences taken from the reading on pages 74-77. Then mark the statements following them T if they are true or F if they are false.

    1. Consequently, the reasoning followed (and still persists among many people) that if urban pollutants could be diluted into the atmosphere at large, the final concentrations would be so low that they would cause no problems.

_____ The subject of the verb *could be diluted* is *urban pollutants*.

_____ The dilution actually took place in the past.

2. Therefore, taller smokestacks—up to 300 meters (1000 feet)—were constructed for many industries and power plants in order to disperse pollutants more widely.

_____ The subject of the verb *were constructed* is *smokestacks*.

_____ The construction took place in the past and continues into the present.

3. Also, power plants have been constructed near coal fields in remote areas to remove their polluting effects from the concentrated areas of cities and instead to disperse them in areas of low pollution.

_____ The subject of the verb *have been constructed* is *coal fields*.

_____ The construction took place in the far distant past.

4. A large power plant may burn 10,000 tons of coal a day; if this coal is contaminated with 3 percent sulfur, some 900 tons of sulfur dioxide per day will be discharged.

_____ The subject of the verb *will be discharged* is *some 900 tons of sulfur dioxide*.

_____ The discharging of the sulfur dioxide will take place in the future.

5. As was noted earlier, in the natural cycle sulfur dioxide may be removed from the air through assimilation by soil microorganisms.

_____ The subject of the verb *may be removed* is *the natural cycle*.

_____ The removal is a process that takes place in the present, will take place in the future, and has taken place in the past.

6. Many statues and monuments have been eroded more in the last 50 years than they had been in the previous 200.

_____ The subject of the verb *have been eroded* is *many statues and monuments*.

_____ The erosion began in the past and goes on into the present.

7. This constitutes a serious loss of fertility, which ultimately must be reflected in a decline in productivity.

_____ The subject of the verb *must be reflected* is *fertility*.

_____ The decline will take place in the future.

8. Unfortunately, because of shortages of high-quality (low-sulfur) oil and natural gas, some leaders in industry and government are asking that air pollution regulations be relaxed to allow the burning of more coal and low-grade oil, which have high sulfur contents.

_____ The subject of the verb *be relaxed* is *air pollution regulations*.

_____ The relaxation is taking place in the present.

9. Another study in the San Bernardino Mountains of California showed that timber production had been reduced by 75 percent.

_____ The subject of the verb *had been reduced* is *another study*.

_____ The reduction took place in the past and continues to take place in the present.

IV. Prediction

EXERCISE

F. Find and copy sentences from the reading on pages 74-77 that use the following thought connectors. Then in the space provided, indicate whether the sentence presents an addition, a result, or a contrast.

in the past	for example (two sentences)
consequently	in addition
therefore (two sentences)	in another study
also	diabolically
however (two sentences)	similarly
as was noted earlier	unfortunately
ironically	obviously
but	another study
thus	many other studies

1. _____

_____

2. _____

_____

3. _____

_____

4. _____

_____

5. _____

_____

6. _____

_____

7. _____

_____

8. _____

_____

9. _____

_____

10. _____

_____

11. _____

_____

12. _____

_____

13. _____

_____

14. _____

_____

15 _____

_____

16. _____

_____

17. _____

_____

18. _____

_____

19. _____

_____

20. _____

_____

21. _____

_____

LESSON SIX
Materials

Textbook Features

Appendix

Textbooks often include one or more appendixes as part of their back matter. An appendix can be used to present a variety of features such as charts, tables, documents, answer sheets, bibliographies, and other reference material that is not essential to the text but is a helpful addition to it. The table of "Controlled Substances of Both Natural and Synthetic Origin" and the "Metric Conversion Chart" in Lesson Two were taken from the appendixes of their respective texts. Although there are no strict rules about what may or may not be included, scientific and technical texts generally contain more items in their appendixes than other kinds of books and journals do. These same types of items sometimes appear on their own (not within an appendix) as various features of a book's back matter.

examples:

appendix a

This is a list of organizations active in environmental matters.* Included here are major national organizations as well as some small, specialized ones. Many of these groups have internship positions available for those wishing to do work in an environmental group. A more complete listing can be found in the Conservation Directory put out by National Wildlife Federation (address below). This Directory includes local, regional, and national organizations; the cost is $4.00.

American Lung Association, 1740 Broadway, New York, N.Y. 10019. Research, education: air pollution effects and means of control.

American Rivers Conservation Council, 317 Pennsylvania Avenue, S.E., Washington, D.C. 20003. Lobbying: wild and scenic rivers.

Center for Renewable Resources, 1001 Connecticut Avenue, N.W., 5th Floor, Washington, D.C. 20036. Research and education: energy policy community organizing on issues concerning renewable resources.

Center for Science in the Public Interest, 1755 S Street, N.W., Washington, D.C. 20009. Research and education: food, nutrition, health.

Citizens Energy Project, 1413 K Street, N.W., Washington, D.C. 20005. Research and education: alternative energy, nuclear power, appropriate technology.

Clean Water Action Project, 1341 G Street, N.W., Suite 200, Washington, D.C. 20005. Lobbying: water quality.

Common Cause, 2030 M Street, N.W., Washington, D.C. 20036. Lobbying: government reform, energy reorganization, clean air.

Concern, Inc., 2233 Wisconsin Avenue, N.W., Washington, D.C. 20007. Research and education: environmental education.

Congress Watch, 133 C Street, S.E., Washington, D.C. 20003. Lobbying: energy.

Conservation Foundation, 1717 Massachusetts Ave., N.W., Washington, D.C. 20036. Research and education: land use, energy conservation, air and water quality.

Consumer Action Now's Council on Environmental Alternatives, 355 Lexington Ave., 16th Floor, New York, N.Y. 10017. Education: energy conservation, solar energy.

Consumer Federation of America, 1012 14th St., N.W., Suite 910, Washington, D.C. 20005. Lobbying: energy policy.

Critical Mass Energy Project, P.O. Box 1538, Washington, D.C. 20013. Research: nuclear power, alternative energy.

Defenders of Wildlife, 1244 19th St., N.W., Washington, D.C. 20036. Research, education and lobbying: endangered species.

Energy Action Educational Foundation, 1523 L Street, N.W., Suite 302, Washington, D.C. 20005. Research and education: consumer energy issues.

Environmental Action Inc., 1346 Connecticut Ave., N.W., Washington, D.C. 20036. Lobbying: transportation, solid waste, water quality, solar energy, energy conservation, toxic substances, deposit legislation.

Environmental Action Foundation, 1346 Connecticut Ave., N.W., Washington, D.C. 20036. Research and education: electric utility rate reform, alternative energy, solid waste, transportation, water quality planning, deposit legislation.

*Adapted with permission from "Where to Write," a list of environmental organizations compiled annually. *Environmental Action,* 10 (May 1979), pp. 15-18; copyright 1979 by Environmental Action, 1346 Connecticut Avenue, N.W., Washington, D.C. 20036. A one-year subscription to the monthly journal is $15.00.

Bernard J. Nebel, *Environmental Science: The Way the World Works* (Englewood Cliffs, N.J.: Prentice-Hall, Inc., 1981), p. 677.

appendix b

the metric system and equivalent english units

LENGTH	1 centimeter (cm) × 10 =	1 decimeter (dm) × 10 =	1 meter (m) × 1000 =	1 kilometer (km)
	= 0.39 inches 1 inch = 2.54 cm	= 3.94 inches 1 foot = 3.05 dm	= 1.09 yards 1 yard = .91 m	= 0.62 miles 1 mile = 1.61 km
AREA	a square 1 cm on each side is	a square 1 m on each side is	100 m by 100 m square or 10,000 m² is	1 km by 1 km square
	1 square centimeter (cm²)	1 square meter (m²)	1 hectare (ha) × 100 =	1 square kilometer (km²)
	= 0.155 square inches 1 square inch = 6.45 cm²	= 10.8 square feet = 1.20 square yards 1 square yard = .836 m²	= 2.47 acres 1 acre = 0.405 ha	= 0.39 square miles 1 square mile = 2.59 km²
VOLUME	a cube 1 cm on each side is	a cube 1 dm on each side is	a cube 1 m on each side is	
	1 cubic centimeter (cc) or 1 milliliter (ml) × 1000 =	1 cubic decimeter (dm) or 1 liter (l) × 1000 =	1 cubic meter or 1 kiloliter (kl)	
	= .203 teaspoons 1 teaspoon = 4.9 ml	= 1.06 quarts 1 quart = .95 l	= 264.2 gallons = 36.5 cubic feet = 28.4 bushels (dry) = 1.31 cubic yards 1 cubic yard = .76 kl	
MASS (WEIGHT)	1 ml of water at 4°C weighs	1 liter of water at 4°C weighs	1 cubic meter of water at 4°C weighs	
	1 gram (g) × 1000 =	1 kilogram (kg) × 1000 =	1 metric ton (t), also called a long ton	
	= .035 ounces 1 ounce = 28.4 g	= 2.2 pounds 1 pound = 0.45 kg	= 2200 pounds = 1.1 short tons 1 short ton (2000 pounds) = .91 t	

Bernard J. Nebel, *Environmental Science: The Way the World Works* (Englewood Cliffs, N.J.: Prentice-Hall, Inc., 1981), p. 680.

Appendix B (cont'd)

energy units and equivalents

1 calorie, food calorie, or kilocalorie—The amount of heat required to raise the temperature of one kilogram of water one degree Celsius (1.8°F).

1 BTU (British Thermal Unit)—The amount of heat required to raise the temperature of one pound of water one degree Fahrenheit.

  1 calorie = 3.968 BTU's
  1 BTU = 0.252 calories

1 therm = 100,000 BTU's
1 quad = 1 quadrillion BTU's

1 watt standard unit of electrical power

  1 watt-hour (wh) = 1 watt for 1 hr. = 3.413 BTU's

1 kilowatt (kw) = 1000 watts

  1 kilowatt-hour (Kwh) = 1 kilowatt for 1 hr. = 3413 BTU's

1 megawatt (Mw) = 1,000,000 watts

  1 megawatt-hour (Mwh) = 1 Mw for 1 hr. = 34.13 therms

1 gigawatt (Gw) = 1,000,000,000 watts or 1,000 megawatts

  1 gigawatt-hour (Gwh) = 1 Gw for 1 hr. = 34,130 therms

1 horsepower = .7457 kilowatts; 1 horsepower-hour = 2545 BTU's

1 cubic foot of natural gas (methane) at atmospheric pressure = 1031 BTU's

1 gallon gasoline = 125,000 BTU's

1 gallon No. 2 fuel oil = 140,000 BTU's

1 short ton coal = 25,000,000 BTU's

1 barrel (oil) = 42 gallons

Bernard J. Nebel, *Environmental Science: The Way the World Works* (Englewood Cliffs, N.J.: Prentice-Hall, Inc., 1981), p. 681.

Answers to Odd-Numbered Problems

CHAPTER 1

1 1%
3 $(1.4 \pm 0.4) \times 10^{10}$ cm^2
5 (a) 1 MV, (b) 1 μm, (c) 40 megadays, (d) 2 kilobucks, (e) 2 nanopieces
7 1 km = 0.621 mi, 1 km/h = 0.621 mi/h.
9 3.3×10^{-10} ft
11 9%
13 (a) 9.5×10^{15} m, (b) 6.3×10^4, (c) 7.2 AU/h
15 m/s^4, m/s^2
17 $T \propto \sqrt{m/k}$

CHAPTER 2

1 50 m
3 (a) 89 km/h, (b) 25 m/s, (c) 81 ft/s
5 (a) 0.19 mi/min, (b) 0
7 (a) $t = 0$ to $t = 20$s, (b) $t \approx 28$s, (c) $t \approx 37$s, (d) both
9 920 km/h
11 3500 cars/h
13 (a)13 m/s, (b) 4.5 m/s away from master
15 (a) 7.5 m, 10.8 m, 11.9 m, (b) 2.2 m/s, (c) 2.2 m/s, 0 m/s
17 3.3 min, 5.0 km; 25 s, 0.62 km
19 4.2 m/s
21 (a) 24 Bt, (b) $A + 300\,B$, 120 B, (c) $A - 3\,Br^4$
23 (a) at t(s) = .12, .37, .62, .87, 1.25, 1.75, etc., v(m/s) = 0.44, 1.40, 2.40, 3.52, 5.36, 7.86, 10.48, 13.14, 15.90, 18.68, 21.44, 23.86, 25.92, 27.80; (b) at t(s) = .06, .25, .50, .75, 1.06, 1.50, 2.00, etc., a(m/s^2) = 3.52, 3.84, 4.00, 4.48, 4.84, 5.00, 5.24, 5.32, 5.52, 5.56, 5.52, 4.84, 4.12, 3.76
25 -2.6 m/s^2
27 391 m
29 (a) 170 m, (b) 14 s, (c) 24 m, 21 m
31 14 g
33 (a) 48 m, (b) 33 m
35 (b) 3.27 s

39 108 km/h
41 (a) 3.6 s, (b) 36 m/s
43 6.4 m/s
45 5.8 s
47 -14 m/s^2
51 (a) 4.8 s, (b) 37 m/s
53 (a) 8.43 m/s, (b) 0.93 s or 2.65 s, (c) first is on the way up, second on the way down
55 56 m
57 9.1 m/s
61 140 m
63 (a) 3.2 $(e^{2t} - 1)$, (b) 1.6 $(e^{2t} - 1)$, (c) $a = 2v + 6.4$, (d) 2.1×10^3 m, 4.3×10^3 m/s
65 (a) $v = (1 - e^{-kt})\, g/k$, (b) g/k

CHAPTER 3

1 Resultant ≈ 6.3 m, 5° S of E
5 1.5
7 (a) 843 km/h N, 537 km/h W; (b) 2530 km N, 1610 km E
9 (7,4,5), 9.5
11 (25 m, 18 m, 36 m), $|\mathbf{D}| = 47$ m
13 (a) 6.7, 27° (b) 4.7, 122°, (c) 7.8, 63°, (d) 8.6, 173°
15 10.5 km/h
17 $v_T/\tan \theta$
19 16.0 km/h
21 (a) 93 m, (b) 110 s
23 32 km/h, 48° N of W
25 43.5° N of E
27 head boat 25° upstream; 37 min
29 Parabola in xz plane at $y = 6.05$
31 (a) 20.0 m/s, 30° N of E, (b) 4.44 m/s^2, 30° S of E, (c) 27.3 m/s; must assume $\mathbf{a}$ = constant.
33 (a) $(-\sin 3.0\ t\mathbf{i} + \cos 3.0\ t\mathbf{j})$(18 m/s), (b) $(-\cos 3.0\ t\mathbf{i} - \sin 3.0\ t\mathbf{j})$(54 m/s^2), (c) circle of radius 6.0 m, (d) $r = -a/9.0$, 180°
35 13 m
37 10.0 m/s
39 12.9 m
41 7.1 s

43 22 m
47 $(v_0 \cos \theta_0/g)(v_0 \sin \theta \pm [v_0^2 \sin^2 \theta_0 - 2gh]^{1/2})$
49 (a) 60 m, (b) 56 m, (c) 34 m/s, $-75°$
51 (a) 3.4 m/s, 48°, (b) 0.32 m above board, (c) 10.5 m/s, 77°
53 $\theta = \phi/2 + \pi/4$
55 8.5 m/s, 118°
57 0.54 m/s^2
59 5.2×10^{-3} m/s^2
61 3.36×10^{-2} m/s^2, $3.4 \times 10^{-3}\ g$
63 (a) 1.86 m/s, (b) 5.50 m/s^2
65 (a_t, a_c) (a) (7.0 m/s^2, 0), (b) (7.0 m/s^2, 25 m/s^2), (c) (7.0 m/s^2, 98 m/s^2)

CHAPTER 4

1 975 N
3 0.020 N
5 3.9×10^2 N
7 2.1×10^4 N; 0.82 m
9 2.0×10^2 N
11 accelerate downward at 1.8 m/s^2
13 (a) 9.6 m/s, (b) 3.6×10^3 N upward
15 6.5 N upward
17 (a) 7.4×10^2 N, (b) 1.3×10^2 N, (c) 6.5×10^2 N, (d) 0
19 (a) 78 N, (b) 2.2×10^2 N, (c) 86 N
21 (a) 4.4 m/s^2, (b) 17 N
23 46 N in top rope, 23 N in bottom rope
25 3.9 m
27 (a) $g(2y - L)/L$, (b) $\sqrt{2gy_0(1 - (y_0/L))}$, (c) $\frac{2}{3}\sqrt{gL}$
29 0.69
31 37 N, 0.54
33 -7.84 m/s^2
35 10.0 kg
37 1.5 m
39 26 m/s
41 (b) 37 m, (c) 220 m
43 12 m/s
45 5.4 m/s^2
47 No

Douglas Giancoli, *General Physics* (Englewood Cliffs, N.J.: Prentice-Hall, Inc., 1984), p. 870.

Appendix

A. Look at two science textbooks. One should be a general introductory text; the other should be an advanced-level or a specialized text on a narrower aspect of a subject. (If you don't have two such texts, find examples in the library or a bookstore). Then check off items on the following list to describe the back matter of these books.

	Text 1	Text 2
1. Does the text have an appendix?	_____	_____
2. Does the text have more than one appendix?	_____	_____
3. Does the appendix include descriptive information?	_____	_____
4. Does the appendix include charts and/or tables?	_____	_____
5. Does the appendix appear important and valuable?	_____	_____
6. If the text has no appendix, does it include a bibliography in the back matter?	_____	_____
7. Does the appendix include answers to problems?	_____	_____
8. Does it include charts and/or tables?	_____	_____
9. Does it include other items?	_____	_____
10. If there are other items in the appendix, what are they?	_____	_____

Glossary

A common feature of textbooks is a glossary. A glossary defines words or phrases unlikely to be known by the general reader. In addition, glossaries define foreign words or phrases and new technical or scientific terms. The words to be defined in a glossary are always presented in alphabetical order, as in a dictionary, for ease in locating them. Each new word or term begins on a new line and is followed by its definition. You can often get an idea of how advanced a text is by looking to see if there is a glossary and by skimming it.

example:

glossary

abiotic. Pertaining to factors or things that are separate and independent from living things; nonliving.

acid. Any compound which releases hydrogen ions when dissolved in water. Also, a water solution which contains a surplus of hydrogen ions.

acid rain. Rainfall that is more acid because of absorption of sulfur dioxide, nitrogen oxides, and certain other pollutants from the air. Sulfur dioxide and nitrogen oxides, respectively, form sulfuric acid and nitric acid.

activated charcoal. A form of carbon that readily adsorbs organic material. Therefore it is frequently used in air and/or water filters to remove organic contaminants. It does not remove ions such as those of the heavy metals.

adaption (ecological or evolutionary). A change in structure or function that produces better adjustment of an organism to its environment, and hence enhances its ability to survive and reproduce.

advanced treatment (sewage treatment). Any of a variety of systems that follow secondary treatment and that are designed to remove one or more nutrients, such as phosphate, from solution.

Bernard J. Nebel, *Environmental Science: The Way the World Works* (Englewood Cliffs, N.J.: Prentice-Hall, Inc., 1981), p. 685.

Glossary

EXERCISE

B. Look at the glossary excerpt on page 100. Then choose a or b to answer these questions about it.

1. Where would a definition of allopolyploidy appear if it were included?
   a. between alkaloids and anaerobic respiration
   b. between aleurone and alkaloids

2. What is the difference between aerobic respiration and anaerobic respiration?
   a. One takes place in an oxygenless environment, while the other requires oxygen to take place.
   b. One is gradual and incomplete, while the other is sudden and complete.

3. What is an example of an alkaloid?
   a. angiosperm
   b. codeine

4. What does ABA stand for?
   a. It is not possible to know from this glossary.
   b. abscisic acid

GLOSSARY

Abscisic acid (ABA) Powerful hormone that acts as an inhibitor, countering the effects of auxins and gibberellins; important factor in seed and tissue dormancy.

Acclimation Gradual physical and biochemical changes that occur in a plant, preparing it to withstand winter conditions.

Acid Substance that when dissolved in water produces a solution in which the H^+ concentration is greater than 10^{-7} M.

Acid rain Rain that has had its pH lowered because of contaminants from industry, such as by combination of sulfur dioxide gas with atmospheric water, forming sulfuric acid.

Aerobic respiration Respiration that occurs in the mitochondria and requires the presence of free oxygen.

Active transport Transport of a substance across a cell membrane with expenditure of energy, such as from a site of lower concentration to a site of higher concentration, against a diffusion gradient.

Adventitious Refers to the development of buds or roots from sites other than their usual organ locations.

Albuminous cell In gymnosperms, unique parenchyma cells (axial and radial) that are closely related to the functioning sieve cells.

Aleurone Outermost cell layer of the endosperm; high in protein and a source of enzymes for the developing seed.

Alkaloids Toxic organic bases found in many plants; colorless, complex in structure, bitter tasting; morphine, codeine, solanine, for example.

Anaerobic respiration Respiration that occurs when oxygen is absent, resulting in incomplete release of energy from glucose; most commonly alcoholic fermentation or lactic acid formation.

Anaphase Stage in mitosis or meiosis where the chromatids of each chromosome separate and move to opposite poles.

Andromedotoxin Toxic substance present in members of the heath family; affects heart and other body systems.

Angiosperm Flowering plant, having seed enclosed in a fruit.

Annual Plant that completes its life cycle in one year.

Anthocyanin Water-soluble pigment in the central vacuole of plant cells; generally red to blue, depending on the pH of the cell sap.

Anthropomorphism Interpretation of what is not human in terms of human or personal characteristics.

Apical dominance Suppression of lateral buds by auxins produced in and translocated downward from the apical bud.

Apical meristems Group of actively dividing cells at tips (apices) of roots and stems.

Apomixis Development of embryo from diploid parental tissue; asexual reproduction not involving meiosis or syngamy (fertilization).

Archegonium (*pl.,* archegonia) Female sex organ containing the egg in bryophytes, lower vascular plants, and gymnosperms.

Ascus (*pl.,* asci) Saclike reproductive structure of ascomycete fungi, producing ascospores.

Roy H. Saigo and Barbara W. Saigo, *Botany: Principles and Applications* (Englewood Cliffs, N.J.: Prentice-Hall, Inc., 1983), p. 507.

5. What level text does this glossary probably come from?
    a. an introductory text
    b. an advanced or specialized text

6. Why are the plural forms of archegonium and ascus included?
    a. because this text is intended for nonnative speakers of English
    b. because these are foreign words that don't form their plurals as English words do

7. What would the phrase "an angry storm" be an example of?
    a. acid rain
    b. anthropomorphism

8. Why did the author probably choose the words included in the glossary?
    a. because they were used in the main body of the textbook and were not defined there
    b. because they are difficult to understand
9. Were any terms defined within the body of the text?
    a. probably
    b. probably not

Index

Another important feature of textbook back matter is the index. Almost all scientific and technical texts contain indexes. The index usually appears last in the back matter because in that position it is easy to locate. The index is usually the most often consulted element of the back matter.

An index is an alphabetical listing of subjects covered in the text. Some indexes are very detailed and include almost everything mentioned in the text, whereas others cite only major ideas that are thoroughly covered within the body of the text.

Index entries are often organized in directory style and alphabetized according to the most important word.

example:

xylem, conduction of water in, 66

The main entries often have subentries, and these often have sub-subentries.

example:

hypertension:
    diet and, 84
    drug therapy of, 85
        in adolescents, 166
    headache and, 85
    idiopathic, 87-88
    pregnancy and, 87
        treatment of, 124
    secondary, 89

example:

INdEX

A

Acceptor (chromatin) site
  for steroid hormones, 74, 432
Accessory reproductive (sex) organs, 383
Acetoacetate (acetoacetic acid), 257
Acetoacetyl-CoA, 257
Acetone:
  formation and ketogenesis, 257
Acetylcholine:
  discovery, 4
  hypothalamus and, 126
  receptors, 68, 321
  structure, 26, 126
Achalasia, 229
Acidophils:
  pituitary, 43, 90

Acinar cells:
  pancreatic, 209, 219, 227, 235
Acne, 397, 412
ACTH (*See* Corticotropin)
Actinomycin D:
  inhibition of hormone action, 52, 53
Activational effects:
  of steroid hormones, 391
Active iodide:
  and thyroid hormone biosynthesis, 297
Acupuncture:
  endorphins and, 493
Addiction:
  endorphins and, 493

Mac E. Hadley, *Endocrinology* (Englewood Cliffs, N.J.: Prentice-Hall, Inc., 1984), p. 529.

Index

EXERCISES

C. Look at a science textbook. Answer the following questions about it.

1. Is there an index? _____

2. Is there more than one index? _____

3. If there is more than one index, what is the difference between (among) them?

    _____

4. How many book pages are occupied by the index? _____

5. Are there any descriptive entries? _____

6. Are all entries just one or two words? _____

7. Are any names of people included? _____

8. Are all entries main entries, or are subentries included? _____

D. Look at the index excerpt below. Respond T if the statements that follow it on page 104 are true, or F if they are false.

INDEX

Shelden H. Radin and Robert T. Folk, *Physics for Scientists and Engineers* (Englewood Cliffs, N.J.: Prentice-Hall, Inc., 1982), p. I1.

_____ 1. There is a section within the text that discusses amplitude in general.

_____ 2. Within the section on air force is a comparison of drag force and air force.

_____ 3. More pages are devoted to Thomson's model of the atom than to Bohr's model.

_____ 4. The availability of thermal energy is mentioned only once in this textbook.

_____ 5. Amperes are mentioned only within the body of the text.

_____ 6. The abbreviation for atmosphere used in this text is *atm*.

_____ 7. This text does not discuss particle accelerators.

_____ 8. Under the main entry for Ampere's law, "applied to a toroid" is a subentry.

_____ 9. The columns of this index are read across, not up and down.

_____ 10. At the top of column 1, *chromatic* is indented under *aberration* because it is a kind of aberration discussed on pages 731 and 733.

_____ 11. Angular momentum is discussed on every page from page 155 to page 161.

_____ 12. Near the top of column 3 the word *and* refers to an electron.

_____ 13. No names of people are mentioned in this index excerpt.

_____ 14. The index indicates the chapter in which each entry is discussed.

_____ 15. A table of contents serves the same purpose as this index.

_____ 16. Batteries are discussed only on pages 500, 505, and 522-23.

_____ 17. If you want general information on angular speed, you have to look on page 76.

_____ 18. Additional information about the adiabatic process can be found by looking elsewhere in this index.

_____ 19. The author assumes that the reader knows the meaning of the abbreviation *ac*.

Reading and Interpreting Charts, Tables, Diagrams, Graphs, Line Drawings, and Schematic Illustrations

The three major kinds of graphs used by authors of scientific and technical prose are circle (or pie) graphs, bar graphs, and line graphs. All graphs compare quantities in one way or another and are used to make information plainly visible in a small amount of space without a lot of descriptive narrative.

Circle Graphs

Circle graphs, more than any other kind of graph, show the relationship of various parts of a whole to each other. In addition, you can see at a glance the relation of the individual parts to the whole.

Authors choose circle graphs when exact quantities are less important than getting a visual feel for the relative quantities of the parts. Sometimes percentages are included and sometimes they are not.

example:

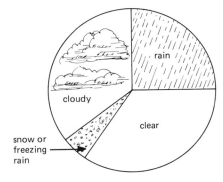

The author of this circle graph did not include percentages in each of the pie-shaped pieces of the circle because she did not think the exact percentages were as important as the general proportions. From looking at this graph, it is apparent that it was clear about as often as it was cloudy and that it rained on fewer days than it was either cloudy or clear. Snow and freezing rain were not nearly so frequent as ordinary rain.

A convenient format for the use of circle graphs is pairs or groups. Two or more circle graphs can quickly transmit a lot of information.

example:

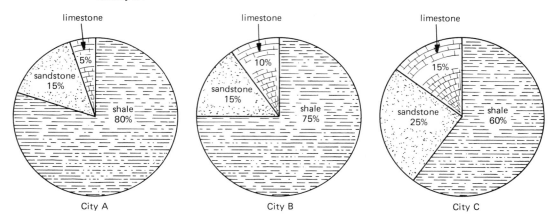

The relative abundance of three kinds of sedimentary rock in three selected southern hemisphere cities

In these examples the author included percentage figures, because the differences were small in some sections and exact quantities could be shown.

Circle Graphs

EXERCISES

E. Look at the pair of circle graphs below. Then complete the statements on page 107.

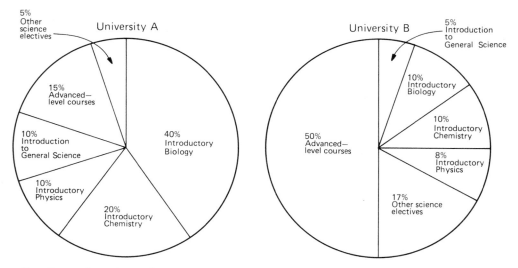

Enrollment in various science courses by first-year students at two midwestern universities

The graph compares (1) _____ enrollments during the students'

(2) _____ year at two (3) _____ . At

University (4) _____ , there is a very different pattern of enrollment

from the one at (5) _____ B. Fully (6) _____ %

of the students at the former take (7) _____ while at the latter

only 10% do. Equal numbers of students at University A take Introductory Physics and

(8) _____ . These two courses at University B account for

(9) _____ % of the total. Advanced-level courses are much more

popular at (10) _____ than at (11) _____ —

more than three times more popular. One of the greatest disparities can be seen in the

(12) _____ category, where fully 17% of the students at Uni-

versity B take these courses. The most striking impression one gets from looking at these

two graphs is the apparently different character of the first-year class at the two

(13) _____ . The students at (14) _____ seem

to be considerably more advanced in science than those at (15) _____ .

F. Rank the first-year science courses at University A and University B in descending
order of popularity. Where percentages are the same, use a bracket ([ ]).

University A	University B
1.	1.
2.	2.
3.	3.
4.	4.
5.	5.
6.	6.

G. Look at the circle graphs below and mark the statements that follow T if they are true or F if they are false.

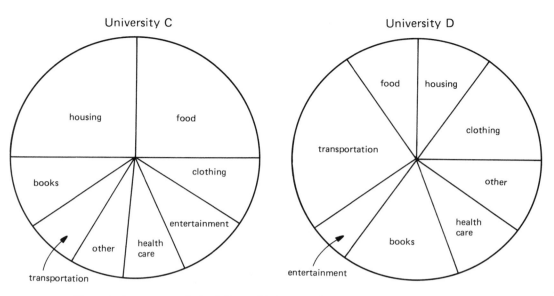

How students spent their dollar at University C and University D last year

_____ 1. Students at University C spent approximately equal amounts of money on food and housing.

_____ 2. Students at University D spent approximately equal amounts of their dollar on food and housing.

_____ 3. Clothing represented one of the larger expenditures of students at both University C and University D.

_____ 4. The graphs show that students at University C spent more dollars on food than students at University D did.

_____ 5. The graphs show that students at University C spent a larger portion of each of their dollars on food than the students at University D did.

_____ 6. The graphs show that the students at University D are richer than those at University C.

_____ 7. The students at University D spent proportionately more on transportation than those at University C.

_____ 8. The graphs demonstrated that students at University C ate more than those at University D.

_____ 9. Books are included in entertainment.

H. Choose a or b to draw conclusions from the graphs in exercise G.

1. Which university probably has more students living at home?
   a. University C
   b. University D

2. Why do you think students at University D spend proportionately more money on transportation?
   a. because they have to travel to the university
   b. because the bus is more expensive

3. Why do students at University D spend proportionately more on books than students at University C?
   a. because they spend less on housing and food
   b. because they read more

4. What expense might be included in the "other" category?
   a. books
   b. tuition (cost of admission to study at the university)

Bar Graphs

Bar graphs are another visual tool used by authors who want to picture data in a convenient form. Bar graphs compare quantities by using vertical or horizontal bars or lines. Authors choose bar graphs instead of pie graphs when the separate quantities, rather than the parts of a whole, are what they want to show.

If the author's interest had been how many students chose which courses at Universities A and B (rather than the percentage of students taking each course), she could have produced a bar graph to present the information.

example:

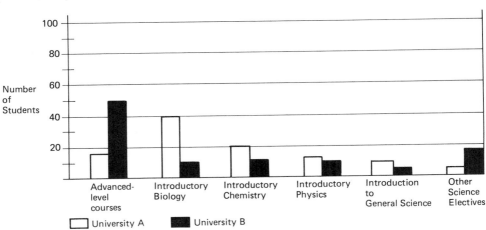

First-year science choices of 108 students at University A and 108 students at University B

Bar Graphs

I. Look at the graph below. Then complete the statements that follow.

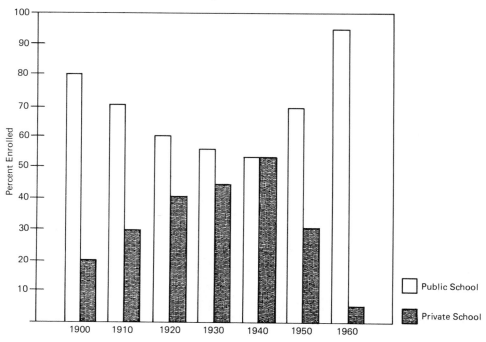

Comparison of school-age population enrolled in public and private schools in Fredonia, 1900 to 1960

1. The bars represent _____ of students enrolled.

2. The data presented in this graph cover a period of _____ years.

3. The population studied in this graph is the _____ population actually attending school.

4. From this graph, we do _____ know how many students actually attended school.

5. The place this study covers is _____ .

6. Except in 1940 enrollment was always highest in _____ school.

7. In _____ enrollment was approximately equal in public and private schools.

8. _____ -school enrollment peaked (was at its highest point) in 1940.

9. The disparity between public-school and private-school enrollment was greatest in ______________________.

10. Proportionately ______________________ students attended private school in 1940 than in 1950.

J. Look at the bar graph below and then choose the letter to best complete each numbered statement.

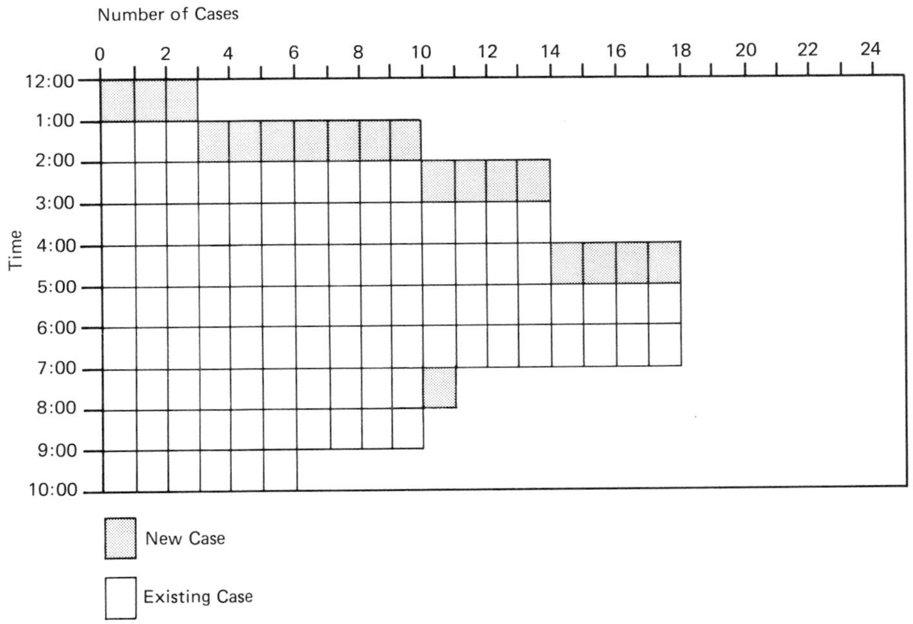

Number of Cases
0
2
4
6
8
10
12
14
16
18
20
22
24
Time
12:00
1:00
2:00
3:00
4:00
5:00
6:00
7:00
8:00
9:00
10:00
New Case
Existing Case

Timetable for cases of food poisoning after 12:00 noon lunch in the university cafeteria

1. The graph covers a period of ______________________ hours.
   a. 24
   b. 10
   c. 19
   d. 12

2. The graph shows ______________________ people got food poisoning after eating in the university cafeteria.
   a. why
   b. how many
   c. where
   d. how

3. It also shows _____ they got sick.
   a. what
   b. how much
   c. which
   d. when

4. One thing the graph does not show is _____.
   a. which cases were new and which were existing
   b. how many people got sick
   c. how many people ate at the cafeteria
   d. when new cases occurred during the indicated time

5. We also do not know _____.
   a. whether there were any new cases after 10:00
   b. what the specific illness was
   c. how many people got sick
   d. where they ate

6. The total number of people who were sick during the ten hours covered by this
   graph is _____.
   a. 123
   b. 19
   c. 10
   d. 24

7. People first began to get sick _____.
   a. at 8:00
   b. between 4:00 and 5:00
   c. at 2:00
   d. right after lunch

8. The time when the greatest number of new cases occurred was

   _____.
   a. between 4:00 and 5:00
   b. between 1:00 and 2:00
   c. impossible to say from the information given
   d. between 5:00 and 6:00

9. A shaded square indicates _____.
   a. food poisoning
   b. a new case
   c. a death
   d. a recovered case

10. The total number of cases peaked (was greatest) _____.
    a. between 1:00 and 2:00
    b. between 12:00 and 1:00
    c. between 4:00 and 7:00
    d. between 9:00 and 10:00

11. The last new case during the time period covered in the graph occurred

_____ .

    a. before 1:00
    b. after 10:00
    c. between 9:00 and 10:00
    d. between 7:00 and 8:00

Earthquake Forecasting and Control

Earthquake in the Peruvian Andes

Man has long wished to predict earthquakes. In fact, every spring a fanatic religious zealot residing in Los Angeles or San Francisco will make such a prediction, giving the day, hour, and minute of the expected **cataclysm**. Although the disappointment is not large when the event fails to occur, man continues to desire the ability to foretell earthquakes, even if the prediction can be made only shortly before the actual fault movement happens.   **1**

Recent findings indicate that reliable earthquake prediction is almost a reality. Before earthquakes occur, there frequently are changes in rock behavior that affect the velocities of other earthquake waves passing through the rocks. Soviet seismologists have used earthquake waves from other unrelated earthquakes to measure the alterations in wave speed through rocks around a fault zone. For   **2**

From William Lee Stokes, Sheldon Judson, and M. Dane Picard, *Introduction to Geology: Physical and Historical*, 2nd ed. (Englewood Cliffs, N.J.: Prentice-Hall, Inc., 1978), pp. 174–175.

months to years before a particular earthquake, Soviet scientists observed that the strained rock in the fault zone **was deformed** in a way that slowed other earthquake waves that passed through the zone. Similar behavior has preceded earthquakes in California and New York.

Changes in electrical resistance, water pressure, rock motion, and leakage of gas also can accompany the lowering of wave velocity. **Fractures** in the fault zone apparently open, which leads to a lowering of water pressure. When the fractures are filled by underground water, the continuing stress on the rocks is also exerted on the water in **pores**, which contributes to the pressure within the rocks and ultimately **triggers further** fault movement and earthquakes.

These preliminary events have been observed and studied for many earthquakes. The larger the earthquake, apparently the longer the time during which the preliminary events take place. Careful observation and measurement of the early events will precede reliable forecasts. The preliminary events are most evident along normal and reverse fault systems, and strike-slip faults may not produce the same effects. Although earthquake forecasting is in its infancy, both American and Soviet scientists have been able to predict the occurrence of a few earthquakes.

Understanding of the causes of earthquakes has opened several possibilities for their control. Underground nuclear explosions in Nevada have released **strain** energy stored in certain rocks. In some instances, the **shock** wave from the explosion has raised the strain on nearby fractures and faults enough to initiate fault movement. All of the resulting earthquakes have been small, but a large earthquake could **conceivably** be initiated.

In the future, a situation may arise where it is desirable to **deliberately** initiate an earthquake near a heavily populated area because too large an amount of strain has accumulated on an active fault zone in the vicinity. If hazardous areas were **evacuated** and if emergency services were standing at the ready, such action might be deemed necessary to prevent a later much more damaging earthquake. However, the legal, environmental, and human problems would be large indeed, perhaps too great for such action to be taken.

Another possibility for earthquake control is much more exciting. Increasing water pressures can initiate faulting, as was **unintentionally** demonstrated by a deep well at the U.S. Army's Rock Mountain Arsenal near Denver, Colorado, in the early 1960s. Disposal of nerve gas wastes in the well triggered movement along deeply buried inactive faults in the region. The liquid waste reduced frictional resistance along fault **planes** in the rocks surrounding the well, leading to movement along the faults. Some of the resulting earthquakes reached magnitudes of 3 and 4 on the Richter scale. Earthquake activity in the area **correlated** closely with the times of pumping

3

4

5

6

7

of wastes into the disposal well, as was demonstrated convincingly by a Denver geologist, David Evans. Strain energy stored along the fault planes was apparently released by the fluid injection.

Experiments by the U.S. Geological Survey in the Rangely oil field of northwestern Colorado have added to the experience gained from the study of the Denver earthquakes. The Survey geologists **8** injected water in some of the Rangely wells, causing very small earthquakes. By **withdrawing** the water, the earthquakes were stopped.

Although it is premature, many geologists believe we **could eventually restrain** earthquakes by injecting fluid into fault zones to permit slippage to take place gradually or in a series of small earth- **9** quakes. However, **means** must be found to control the areas affected and to be certain a major destructive quake is not triggered.

Vocabulary

cataclysm (noun)

immense earthquake; natural disaster; catastrophe

In fact, every spring a fanatic religious zealot residing in Los Angeles or San Francisco will make such a prediction, giving the day, hour, and minute of the expected **cataclysm**.

to deform (verb)

to alter the normal shape of something by the application of stress

For months to years before a particular earthquake, the Soviet scientists observed that the strained rock in the fault zone **was deformed** in a way that slowed other earthquake waves that passed through the zone.

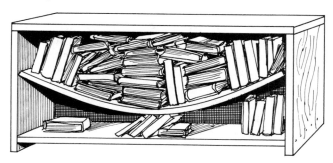

fracture (noun)

crack; break; opening

Fractures in the fault zone apparently open, which leads to a lowering of water pressure.

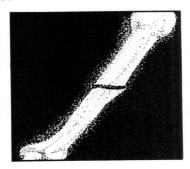

pore (noun)

natural opening through which liquid or gas can travel

When the fractures are filled by underground water, the continuing stress on the rocks is also exerted on the water in **pores**, which contributes to the pressure within the rocks and ultimately triggers further fault movement.

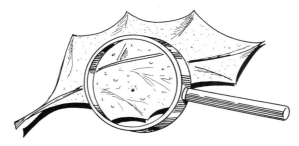

to trigger (verb)

to initiate; to cause

When the fractures are filled by underground water, the continuing stress on the rocks is also exerted on the water in pores, which contributes to the pressure within the rocks and ultimately **triggers** further fault movement.

further (adjective)

additional

When the fractures are filled by underground water, the continuing stress on the rocks is also exerted on the water in pores, which contributes to the pressure within the rocks and ultimately triggers **further** fault movement.

strain (noun)

stress; pressure

Underground nuclear explosions in Nevada have released **strain** energy stored in certain rocks.

shock (noun)

sudden, violent blow or jolt, as from an explosion or earthquake

In some instances, the **shock** wave from the explosion has raised the strain on nearby fractures and faults enough to initiate fault movement.

conceivably (adverb)

possibly; imaginably

All of the resulting earthquakes have been small, but a large earthquake could **conceivably** be initiated.

deliberately (adverb)

on purpose

In the future, a situation may arise where it is desirable to **deliberately** initiate an earthquake near a heavily populated area because too large an amount of strain has accumulated on an active fault zone in the vicinity.

to evacuate (verb)

to empty deliberately, especially of people

If hazardous areas were **evacuated** and if emergency services were standing at the ready, such action might be deemed necessary to prevent a later much more damaging earthquake.

unintentionally (adverb)

not deliberately

Increasing water pressures can initiate faulting, as was **unintentionally** demonstrated by a deep well at the U.S. Army's Rocky Mountain Arsenal near Denver, Colorado, in the early 1960s.

plane (noun)

flat surface

The liquid waste reduced frictional resistance along fault **planes** in the rocks surrounding the well, leading to movement along the faults.

to correlate (verb)

> to link; to connect; to relate together

> Earthquake activity in the area **correlated** closely with the times of pumping of wastes into the disposal well, as was demonstrated convincingly by a Denver geologist, David Evans.

to withdraw (verb)

> to take out; to remove

> By **withdrawing** the water, the earthquakes were stopped.

eventually (adverb)

> at some unknown time in the future

> Although it is premature, many geologists believe we could **eventually** restrain earthquakes by injecting fluid into fault zones to permit slippage to take place gradually or in a series of small earthquakes.

to restrain (verb)

> to limit; to reduce the intensity or frequency of

> Although it is premature, many geologists believe we **could** eventually **restrain** earthquakes by injecting fluid into fault zones to permit slippage to take place gradually or in a series of small earthquakes.

means (noun)

> way(s); method(s)

> However, **means** must be found to control the areas affected and to be certain a major destructive quake is not triggered.

Vocabulary Exercises

A. Choose the response that best completes each of the following statements.

1. This was _____ the worst cataclysm in modern history.
   a. unintentionally
   b. deliberately
   c. conceivably
   d. eventually

2. We _____ our hand immediately through a reflex response if we touch something very hot.
   a. restrain
   b. withdraw
   c. correlate
   d. evacuate

3. There are several _____ of treating hypertension.
   a. means
   b. planes
   c. shocks
   d. strains

4. Brakes are used to _____ the speed of many moving vehicles.
   a. deform
   b. withdraw
   c. restrain
   d. correlate

5. Something that was not done deliberately can be said to have been done

   _____ .
   a. conceivably
   b. eventually
   c. further
   d. unintentionally

6. _____ of gas from appliances can be very dangerous.
   a. Leakage
   b. Strain
   c. Pores
   d. Cataclysms

7. Almost any substance can be _____ by great pressure or heat.
   a. evacuated
   b. deformed
   c. correlated
   d. withdrawn

8. _____ (some say by the year 2000), electric vehicles will be very common.
   a. Eventually
   b. Deliberately
   c. Unintentionally
   d. Fracture

9. Sometimes a great cataclysm takes place before it is possible to

_____ anyone.
   a. restrain
   b. evacuate
   c. deform
   d. trigger

10. We don't know if excessive sodium consumption causes high blood pressure, but we

do know that the two are often _____ .
   a. deformed
   b. restrained
   c. triggered
   d. correlated

11. A floor is an example of a _____ .
   a. shock
   b. plane
   c. strain
   d. pore

12. A great _____ can take hundreds of thousands of lives.
   a. cataclysm
   b. pore
   c. means
   d. fracture

B. Replace the italicized word or phrase in each of the sentences below with a word from the vocabulary list.

1. It is not known if one event can *cause* a heart attack.
2. We are awaiting *additional* information about the damage the earthquake caused.
3. Plants have *holes* almost too small to be seen.
4. Great stress can cause *cracks* in solid rock.
5. The *stress* exerted on rocks in fault zones can be tremendous.
6. It is not yet known if giant earthquakes can be triggered *on purpose*.
7. The *jolts* from the earthquake could be felt hundreds of kilometers away.

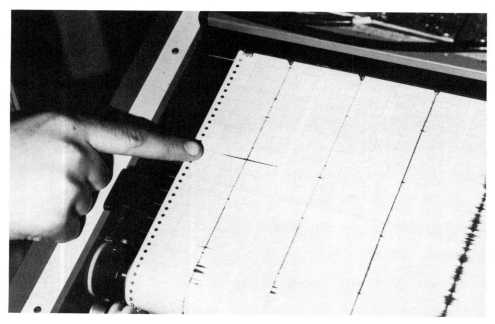

Seismic tracing showing an earthquake
Russ Kinne, Photo Researchers, Inc.

Comprehension

I. Meaning

EXERCISE

C. Complete each of the following statements with *one* word taken from the reading on pages 114-116.

1. _____ prediction is common and not new.

2. The _____ to predict earthquakes continues to be desired.

3. Accurate predictions are currently virtually a _____ .

4. Alterations in rock behavior which affect the speeds at which other seismic _____ pass through rocks precede major quakes.

5. Also, according to Soviet and American scientists, rocks have been _____ , slowing unrelated seismic waves that passed through the zone.

6. This has happened before _____ that occurred both in New York and California.

7. The other factor that accompanies the slowing of seismic wave speed is gas
   _____.

8. It is thought that the lowering of _____ pressure is caused by the opening of fractures.

9. This allows the fractures to fill with _____.

10. Additional _____ movement is in turn caused by increased pressure within the rocks.

11. When a great cataclysm is to occur, the changes in electrical resistance, water pressure, rock motion, leakage of gas, and lowering of wave velocity take place over a long period of _____.

12. In order to predict earthquakes reliably, it is necessary to observe and measure the preliminary _____ carefully.

13. Not all kinds of fault _____ exhibit these preliminary events.

14. _____ faults, for example, do not evidence these features.

15. In spite of the fact that not everything is known about earthquake predicting, the _____ of some earthquakes has been accurately forecast.

16. Because we have begun to appreciate the factors involved in earthquake causation, _____ has become a possibility.

17. The discovery that strain energy could be released was made following underground _____ testing.

18. The explosion causes a _____ wave.

19. This wave has been observed to _____ rock movement along fault lines.

20. Although these _____ have not been cataclysms, it is possible that larger quakes could have been triggered.

21. Eventually, it is possible that the intentional triggering of an earthquake might be _____.

22. This would probably be considered only in an area that is densely _____.

23. This would be undertaken in order to _____ an even larger earthquake from occurring later.

24. Faults can be formed by _____ water pressure.

25. The water apparently reduces friction and thereby causes rock

_____ .

26. It appears that the earthquakes can be _____ by withdrawing the fluid that was injected.

27. Many geologists feel that this method of _____ fluid into fault zones could some day be used to ease pressure.

28. It is still premature to count on this method, because it is not yet known how to

_____ the movement set off by the fluid injection.

II. Reference

EXERCISE

D. Choose a or b to indicate the reference for the italicized word in each numbered statement taken from the reading on pages 114-116. Paragraph numbers are given.

1. In fact, every spring a fanatic religious zealot residing in Los Angeles or San Francisco will make *such a prediction*, giving the day, hour, and minute of the expected cataclysm. (¶ 1)
   a. of an earthquake
   b. of a religious event

Reading and interpreting seismograms
U.S. Geological Survey

2. Although the disappointment is not large when *the event* fails to occur, man continues to desire the ability to foretell earthquakes, even if the prediction can be made only shortly before the actual fault movement happens. (¶ 1)
   a. the cataclysm
   b. the disappointment

3. For months to years before a particular earthquake, Soviet scientists observed that the strained rock in *the fault zone* was deformed in a way that slowed other earthquake waves that passed through the zone. (¶ 2)
   a. the zone of the quake
   b. the zone of other earthquake waves

4. *Similar behavior* has preceded earthquakes in California and New York. (¶ 2)
   a. earthquake prediction
   b. deformation of rocks in areas where a quake will occur

5. When the fractures are filled by underground water, the continuing stress on the rocks is also exerted on the water in pores, *which* contributes to the pressure within the rocks and ultimately triggers further fault movement and earthquakes. (¶ 3)
   a. increased stress on water in pores
   b. pores

6. *These preliminary events* have been observed and studied for many earthquakes. (¶ 4)
   a. predictions
   b. rock deformation, changes in electrical resistance, water pressure, rock motion, and leakage of gas

7. The preliminary events are most evident along normal and reverse fault systems, and strike-slip faults may not produce *the same effects.* (¶ 4)
   a. the preliminary events
   b. normal and reverse fault systems

8. All of *the resulting earthquakes* have been small, but a large earthquake could conceivably be initiated. (¶ 5)
   a. those triggered by underground explosions
   b. those in nearby fractures

9. If hazardous areas were evacuated and if emergency services were standing at the ready, *such action* might be deemed necessary to prevent a later much more damaging earthquake. (¶ 6)
   a. deliberate triggering of an earthquake
   b. evacuation of people and readying of emergency services

10. The liquid waste reduced frictional resistance along fault planes in the rocks surrounding *the well*, leading to movement along the faults. (¶ 7)
    a. in which an earthquake was intentionally triggered
    b. in which nerve gas wastes were disposed of

11. Earthquake activity in *the area* correlated closely with the times of pumping of wastes into the disposal well, as was demonstrated convincingly by a Denver geologist, David Evans. (¶ 7)
    a. of the well
    b. of the earthquakes

III. Syntax: -ing Words (Gerunds, Participles, Progressives)

EXERCISE

E. Choose the paraphrase closer in meaning to each italicized phrase containing an *-ing* word. The sentences come from the reading on pages 114–116.

1. In fact, every spring a fanatic religious zealot residing in Los Angeles or San Francisco will make such a prediction, *giving the day, hour, and minute of the expected cataclysm.*
   a. which gives the day, hour, and minute of the expected cataclysm
   b. while giving the day, hour, and minute of the expected cataclysm

2. Before earthquakes occur, there frequently are changes in rock behavior that affect the velocities of other earthquake waves *passing through rocks.*
   a. that rocks pass through
   b. that pass through rocks

3. Changes in electrical resistance, water pressure, rock motion, and leakage of gas also can accompany *the lowering of wave velocity.*
   a. the slowdown of wave velocity
   b. while lowering wave velocity

4. When the fractures are filled by underground water, *the continuing stress* on the rocks is also exerted on the water in pores, which contributes to the pressure within the rocks and ultimately triggers further fault movement and earthquakes.
   a. the stress that continues
   b. while the stress continues

5. Although *earthquake forecasting* is in its infancy, both American and Soviet scientists have been able to predict the occurrence of a few earthquakes.
   a. earthquakes that forecast
   b. the forecasting of earthquakes

6. *Understanding of* the causes of earthquakes has opened several possibilities for their control.
   a. The fact that we understand
   b. When understanding

7. All of *the resulting earthquakes* have been small, but a large earthquake could conceivably be initiated.
   a. the earthquakes that have resulted
   b. the results of the earthquakes

8. If hazardous areas were evacuated and if emergency services were standing at the ready, such action might be deemed necessary to prevent a later *much more damaging earthquake.*
   a. an earthquake capable of causing more damage
   b. a more damaged earthquake

A seismogram made at a depth of 100 meters forms part of a worldwide seismograph network.
U.S. Geological Survey

9. *Increasing water pressures can initiate faulting*, as was unintentionally demonstrated by a deep well at the U.S. Army's Rocky Mountain Arsenal near Denver, Colorado, in the early 1960s.
   a. Water pressures that increase can cause faults
   b. While increasing water pressures, faulting can initiate

10. The liquid waste reduced frictional resistance along fault planes in the rocks *surrounding the well* . . .
    a. which surround the well
    b. while surrounding the well

Earthquake in Romania
U.S. Geological Survey

11. ... *leading to movement along the faults.*
    a. leading movement along the faults
    b. and lead to movement along the faults

12. Earthquake activity in the area correlated closely with the times of *pumping of wastes* into the disposal well, as was demonstrated convincingly by a Denver geologist, David Evans.
    a. waste pumping
    b. pumps that were wasted

13. The Survey geologists injected water in some of the Rangely wells, *causing very small earthquakes.*
    a. which caused very small earthquakes
    b. while causing very small earthquakes

14. *By withdrawing the water*, the earthquakes were stopped.
    a. While the water was withdrawn
    b. Because of the withdrawal of the water

IV. Prediction: Topic Sentences

EXERCISE

F. Section a consists of topic sentences taken from the reading. Paragraph numbers are indicated. Put each invented sentence listed in section b into the appropriate paragraph by matching it with the topic sentence.

section a

1. Man has long wished to predict earthquakes. (¶ 1)

_____

_____

2. Recent findings indicate that reliable earthquake prediction is almost a reality. (¶ 2)

_____

_____

3. Understanding of the causes of earthquakes has opened several possibilities for their control. (¶ 5) _____

_____

4. Experiments by the U.S. Geological Survey in the Rangely oil field of northwestern Colorado have added to the experience gained from the study of the Denver earthquakes. (¶ 8) _____

_____

5. Although it is premature, many geologists believe we could eventualy restrain earthquakes by injecting fluid into fault zones. (¶ 9)

_____

_____

section b

Several small quakes have been successfully predicted in the last few years.

In ancient times, it was believed that certain cloud patterns foretold seismic activity.

Many implementation problems would have to be overcome, but the future looks brighter than it ever has.

In several of these the effects were virtually duplicated.

Two methods are being investigated in the laboratory.

LESSON EIGHT
Materials

Textbook Features

Bibliographies and Reference Lists

Most textbooks and journals provide bibliographies, reference lists, and other indications of sources that were consulted by the author(s) or that are recommended to the reader.

The main difference between a bibliography and a reference list is that a bibliography is more general and contains many works that were not cited or referred to in the text. A reference list, on the other hand, provides the reader with a thorough listing of books and journal articles referred to in the text. Often authors of scientific and technical material will make a statement such as this:

The term *magma* (Greek, "paste") was first applied in geological usage by G. P. Scrope, who introduced a pharmaceutical word for ointment to emphasize "its analogy to those compound liquids such as mud, paste, milk, blood, honey, etc., which consist of solid particles deriving a certain freedom of motion amongst one another from their intimate admixture, in greater or less proportion, with one or more perfect fluids, which act as their vehicle" (Scrope, 1825, p. 19, as quoted by Simkin, 1967, pp. 66-67).

Daniel S. Barker, *Igneous Rocks*
(Englewood Cliffs, N.J.: Prentice-Hall, Inc., 1983), p. 1.

You can expect to find elsewhere in that same book a reference list giving bibliographic information on Scrope's 1825 work and Simkin's 1967 work. That information is included to help you find those works in a library in case you want to see them in their entirety. A bibliography may also be included, whether or not the book contains a reference list.

Authors refer to bibliographies and reference lists by several names: Bibliography, Select Bibliography, References, Works Cited, Sources, Suggested Readings, and others. They usually appear in the back matter, often as the last feature before the index. In many scientific and technical works, however, especially teaching texts, professional journals, and other heavily documented works, the bibliography (or more often the reference list) is placed at the end of the chapter to which it belongs.

Bibliographies included in textbooks (rather than those published separately and meant to be comprehensive) do not generally list all material available in the subject covered. The author selects those works he or she considers to be of interest or use to the reader. If the text covers many areas of a large subject (as an introductory college text does) the bibliography may include works of related interest in the various subdivisions of that field. Often the author includes a statement at the beginning of the bibliography explaining the rationale for the inclusion of the works selected or the organization of the list as a whole.

Remember that bibliographies and reference lists are not footnotes or notes, which give the exact location of direct quotations or paraphrases of material taken from other works. These will be covered in Lesson Ten.

There are several ways to organize bibliographies and reference lists, including the following.

alphabetical by author's last name
divided by subject matter
divided by types of material (sectional)
annotated

Bibliographies and Reference Lists

EXERCISE

A. Look at your biggest textbook. Find all bibliographies and reference lists and then choose the responses that answer each of the following questions.

1. What does your book have?
   a. bibliography only
   b. reference list only
   c. bibliography and reference list
   d. neither

2. Where do these features appear?
   a. in the back matter
   b. within the text itself
   c. in the front matter
   d. at the bottom of pages

3. What precedes the bibliography?
   a. nothing
   b. a statement of explanation
   c. something other than an explanation
   d. heads only

4. How is the bibliography organized?
   a. alphabetically by author's last name
   b. divided by subject matter
   c. divided by types of material
   d. some combination of a, b, and c

More About Bibliographies and Reference Lists

Since science journals and texts often contain lengthy bibliographies and reference lists, it is helpful to understand the organization followed by most authors. Basically, the same information is found in all bibliographies and reference lists, although individual ones may present these data in varying order and in different styles. Many of the items listed below (such as series title) may not be applicable in every case, but when they are applicable, they are included in the listing. In books the following information is given.

name of author(s) (may be an editor or an institution)

title, subtitle, series title

edition

volume number

publisher's name

place of publication

date of publication

If the listing is for an article in a journal, the following additional information is included if applicable.

title of article

name of publication

volume number

pages on which the article appears

date of the issue

Most bibliographies are arranged in alphabetical order by author's last name, either through the whole list or within the various sections of a divided list.

In both bibliographies and reference lists, multiple works by the same author are arranged chronologically. After the first listing, the author's name is replaced by a long dash.

example:

Barrington, E. J. W. 1964. *Hormones and evolution.* London: The English Universities Press, Ltd.

_____ . 1975. *An introduction to general and comparative endocrinology.* 2nd ed. London: Oxford University Press, Inc.

Mac E. Hadley, *Endocrinology* (Englewood Cliffs, N.J.: Prentice-Hall, Inc., 1984), p. 526.

If two works written by an author in the same year appear in a reference list, they are generally lettered consecutively to distinguish them when they are referred to in the text and in the reference list.

example:

(*text*)

Some new research points to the predictability of tremors in areas of low seismic activity (Greene, 1984b)

(*reference list*)

Greene, Marianne R. 1984a. *Geology Today.* Trenton, N.J.: Smith Press

_____ 1984b. *Seismic Activity.* New York: Jones Publishing Co.

A work written by one author comes before a work written by that same author with a co-author.

example:

Blatt, H., 1982. *Sedimentary Petrology.* W. H. Freeman, San Francisco, 555 pp. Excellent treatment of the subject. The best book on petrology of sedimentary rocks currently available.

Blatt, H., Middleton, G. V., and Murray, R. C., 1980. *Origin of Sedimentary Rock*, 2nd ed. Prentice-Hall, Englewood Cliffs, N.J., 782 p. (Chapters 2, 8, 9, and 12-19). In some respects this book is a companion volume to the present book. The suggested chapters expand considerably on the subjects treated in the preceding chapter of this book.

Richard A. David, Jr., *Depositional Systems:*
A Genetic Approach to Sedimentary Geology
(Englewood Cliffs, N.J.: Prentice-Hall, Inc., 1983), p. 33.

When more than two authors are responsible for a book cited in the text, it is customary to cite only the first author's name followed by *et al.* or *and others*. The corresponding reference list then lists all the authors in the order in which they appear on that book's title page.

example:

(*text*)

Applied research in FBC boiler technology has shown a 60% reduction in overall pollution emissions (Rosen et al. 1978).

(*reference list*)

Rosen, Jill, B., Choi, Timothy R., and Zannieri, Maria, 1978. Ann. of Boiler Tech. 7:1-9.

Reference lists in scientific journals (and sometimes in books as well) have a slightly different style. These lists commonly shorten the titles of other scientific periodicals in the interest of saving space. It is assumed that the reader is a specialist in the subject and will therefore be familiar with other journals dealing with this field.

examples:

Griffin, D. M. 1963. Soil physical factors and the ecology of fungi III. Activity of fungi in relatively dry soil. Trans. Brit, Mycol. Soc. **46**:373-377

————. 1969. Soil water in the ecology of fungi. Ann. Rev. Phytopathol. 7:289-310.

Elizabeth Moore-Landecker, *Fundamentals of the Fungi*, 2nd ed.
(Englewood Cliffs, N.J.: Prentice-Hall, Inc., 1982), p. 437.

Many textbooks offer annotated bibliographies. Annotations are most often included when the bibliography appears within the textbook itself at the end of chapters. These annotated bibliographies are often entitled "Readings," "Suggested Readings," or some variant of these. In an annotated bibliography the author offers a concise evaluation or characterization of each listed work. This type of bibliography is very helpful since it can indicate to the reader interested in research whether it is worth searching for a particular work in the library. The example taken from *Depositional Systems* on page 141 of this text shows how authors sometimes annotate a bibliography.

Bibliographies and Reference Lists

EXERCISES

B. Look at the excerpts from the sectional bibliography on page 136. Then mark these statements T if they are true or F if they are false.

_____ 1. This is a reference list.

_____ 2. The entire bibliography is arranged alphabetically by author in one list.

_____ 3. This list is divided by types of works.

_____ 4. Its major divisions are chronological.

_____ 5. A monograph is a serial publication.

_____ 6. *Advances in Prostaglandin and Thromboxane Research* is the title of an article in an endocrinology-related journal.

_____ 7. There are two books listed for which E. H. Frieden is the sole author.

_____ 8. There are two books listed for which E. J. W. Barrington is the sole author.

_____ 9. The "Books and Monographs" section is in chronological rather than alphabetical order.

_____ 10. Where one author has written more than one book, these are listed in chronological order.

_____ 11. *Endocrinol. Jap.* is the title of a journal.

C. Look at the reference list on page 137. Then choose a or b to answer each of the following numbered questions.

1. How many works on this list were written, at least in part, by R. N. Anderson?
   a. 1
   b. 7

2. How many different authors are represented on this list?
   a. 14
   b. 11

3. What are these references to?
   a. books and monographs
   b. journals and serial publications

4. How was the Allègre, Dupré, Lambret, and Richard referred to when it appeared in the text?
   a. Allègre, Dupré, and Richard
   b. Allègre et al.

5. Where was O. L. Anderson's article published?
   a. in *Proc. Second Internat. Kimberlite Conference*
   b. in *Jour. Geology*

Note: This bibliography has been shortened.

Bibliography

BOOKS AND MONOGRAPHS

BARRINGTON, E. J. W. 1964. *Hormones and evolution.* London: The English Universities Press, Ltd.

_____. 1975. *An introduction to general and comparative endocrinology.* 2nd ed. London: Oxford University Press, Inc.

BENTLEY, P. J. 1982. *Comparative vertebrate endocrinology,* 2nd ed. Cambridge, England: Cambridge University Press.

DeGROOT, L. J., G. F. CAHILL, JR., L. MARTINI, D. H. NELSON, W. D. ODELL, J. T. POTTS, JR., E. STEINBERGER, and A. I. WINEGRAD, eds. 1979. *Endocrinology,* vols. 1–3. New York: Grune & Stratton, Inc.

FRIEDEN, E. H. 1976. *Chemical endocrinology.* New York: Academic Press, Inc.

FRIEDEN, E. H., and H. LIPNER. 1971. *Biochemical endocrinology of the vertebrates.* Englewood Cliffs, N.J.: Prentice Hall Publishing Co., Inc.

FRYE, B. E. 1967. *Hormonal control in vertebrates.* New York: Macmillan, Inc.

* * *

MAJOR ENDOCRINOLOGY JOURNALS

Acta Endocrinologica (Acta Endocrinol.)
Advances In Cyclic Nucleotide Research (Advan. Cyclic Nucl. Res.)
Annales d'Endocrinologie (Ann. d'Endocrinol.)
Clinical Endocrinology (Clin. Endocrinol.)
Endocrine Research Communications (Endoc. Res. Commun.)
Endocrinologica Japonica (Endocrinol. Jap.)

* * *

ENDOCRINOLOGY-RELATED JOURNALS

Advances In Prostaglandin and Thromboxane Research
Advances In Steroid Biochemistry and Pharmacology
American Journal of Physiology (Am. J. Physiol.)
Cell and Tissue Research (Cell Tissue Res.)
Clinical Investigation (Clin. Invest.)
Diabetes
FEBS Letters

* * *

SERIAL PUBLICATIONS

Annual Review of Biochemistry (Ann. Rev. Biochem.)
Annual Review of Medicine (Ann. Rev. Med.)
Annual Review of Neuroscience (Ann. Rev. Neurosci.)
Annual Review of Pharmacology and Toxicology (Ann. Rev. Pharmacol. Toxicol.)
Annual Review of Physiology (Ann. Rev. Physiol.)

Mac E. Hadley, *Endocrinology* (Englewood Cliffs, N.J.: Prentice-Hall, Inc., 1984), pp. 526–528.

References

Allègre, C. J., and D. Ben Othman, 1980, "Nd–Sr isotopic relationship in granitoid rocks and continental crust development: a chemical approach to orogenesis," *Nature, 286,* 335–342.

Allègre, C. J., and J.-F. Minster, 1978, "Quantitative models of trace element behavior in magmatic processes," *Earth and Planetary Science Letters, 38,* 1–25.

Allègre, C. J., B. Dupré, B. Lambret, and P. Richard, 1981, "The subcontinental versus suboceanic debate: 1. Lead–neodymium–strontium isotopes in primary alkali basalts from a shield area: the Ahaggar volcanic suite," *Earth and Planetary Science Letters, 52,* 85–92.

Anderson, A. T., 1974, "Chlorine, sulfur and water in magmas and oceans," *Geol. Soc. America Bulletin, 85,* 1485–1492.

Anderson, A. T., 1975, "Some basaltic and andesitic gases," *Reviews of Geophysics and Space Physics, 13,* 37–55.

Anderson, A. T., 1976, "Magma mixing: petrological process and volcanological tool," *Jour. Volcanol. and Geothermal Research, 1,* 3–33.

Anderson, D. L., 1979, "The deep structure of continents," *Jour. Geophys. Research, 84,* 7555–7560.

Anderson, D. L., 1981, "Rise of deep diapirs," *Geology, 9,* 7–9.

Anderson, O. L., 1979, "The role of fracture dynamics in kimberlite pipe formation," *Proc. Second Internat. Kimberlite Conference, 1,* 344–353.

Anderson, R. N., S. E. DeLong, and W. M. Schwarz, 1980, "Dehydration, asthenospheric convection and seismicity in subduction zones," *Jour. Geology, 88,* 445–451.

Appleyard, E. C., and A. R. Woolley, 1979, "Fenitization: an example of the problems of characterizing mass transfer and volume changes," *Chemical Geology, 26,* 1–15.

Daniel S. Barker, *Igneous Rocks* (Englewood Cliffs, N.J.: Prentice-Hall, Inc., 1983), p. 373.

D. Look at the partial reference list below and on page 139. Then answer the questions that follow on page 140.

References

Alexander, M. 1977. Introduction to soil microbiology, Second ed. John Wiley & Sons, Inc., New York. 467 pp.

Allcroft, R. 1969. Aflatoxicosis in farm animals. *In:* Goldblatt, L. A., Ed., Aflatoxin—scientific background, control and implications. Academic Press, New York. pp. 237-264.

Barton, R. 1960. Antagonism amongst some sugar fungi. *In:* Parkinson, D., and J. S. Waid, Eds., The ecology of soil fungi: an international symposium. Liverpool University Press, Liverpool. pp. 160-167.

Birch, L. C., and D. P. Clark. 1953. Forest soil as an ecological community with special reference to fauna. Quart. Rev. Biol. **28:**13-36.

Brian, P. W. 1951. Antibiotics produced by fungi. Botan. Rev. **17:**357-430.

——, 1960. Antagonistic and competitive mechanisms limiting survival and activity of fungi in soil. *In:* Parkinson, D., and J. S. Waid, Eds., The ecology of soil fungi: an international symposium. Liverpool University Press, Liverpool. pp. 115-129.

Broadbent, D. 1966. Antibiotics produced by fungi. Botan. Rev. **32:**219-242.

Brook, P. J., and E. P. White. 1966. Fungus toxins affecting mammals. Ann. Rev. Phytopathology **4:**171-194.

Burges, A. 1965. The soil microflora—its nature and biology. *In:* Baker, K. F., and W. C. Snyder, Eds., Ecology of soil-borne plant pathogens—prelude to biological control. University of California Press, Berkeley, Los Angeles, Calif. pp. 21-32.

——. 1967. The decomposition of organic matter in the soil. *In:* Burges, A., and F. Raw, Eds., Soil biology. Academic Press, New York. pp. 479-492.

——, and E. Fenton. 1953. The effect of carbon dioxide on the growth of certain soil fungi. Trans. Brit. Mycol. Soc. **36:**104-108.

——, and P. Latter. 1960. Decomposition of humic acid by fungi. Nature **186:**404-405.

Chen, A. W., and D. M. Griffin. 1966. Soil physical factors and the ecology of fungi. VI. Interaction between temperature and soil moisture. Trans. Brit. Mycol. Soc. **49:**551-561.

Chesters, C. G. C., and R. H. Thornton. 1956. A comparison of techniques for isolating soil fungi. Trans. Brit. Mycol. Soc. **39:**301-313.

Christensen, C. M., and H. H. Kaufmann. 1965. Deterioration of stored grains by fungi. Ann. Rev. Phytopathol. **3:**69-84.

Clark, F. E. 1965. The concept of competition in microbial ecology. *In:* Baker, K. F., and W. C. Snyder. Eds., Ecology of soil-borne plant pathogens—prelude to biological control. University of California Press, Berkeley, Los Angeles, Calif. pp. 339-347.

Diener, U. L., and N. D. Davis. 1969. Aflatoxin formation by *Aspergillus flavus*. *In:* Goldblatt, L. A., Ed., Aflatoxin—scientific background, control and implications. Academic Press, New York. pp. 13-54.

Dobbs, C. G., W. H. Hinson, and J. Bywater. 1960. Inhibition of fungal growth in soils. *In:* Parkinson, D., and J. S. Waid, Eds., The ecology of soil fungi: an international symposium. Liverpool University Press, Liverpool. pp. 130-147.

Feuell, A. J. 1969. Types of mycotoxins in foods and feeds. *In:* Goldblatt, L. A., Ed., Aflatoxin—scientific background, control and implications. Academic Press, New York. pp. 187-222.

Flaig, W., H. Beutelspacher, and E. Rietz. 1975. Chemical composition and physical properties of humic substances. *In:* Gieseking, J. E., Ed., Soil components—organic components. Springer-Verlag, New York. **1**:1–211.

Forgacs, J., and W. T. Carll. 1962. Mycotoxicoses. Advan. Veterinary Sci. **7**:274–382.

Garrett, S. D. 1950. Ecology of the root-inhabiting fungi. Biol. Rev. **25**:220–254.

——. 1951. Ecological groups of soil fungi: a survey of substrate relationships. New Phytologist **50**:159–166.

——. 1955. Microbial ecology of the soil. Trans. Brit. Mycol. Soc. **38**:1–9.

——. 1963. Soil fungi and soil fertility. The Macmillan Co., New York. 165 pp.

Gascoigne, J. A., and M. M. Gascoigne. 1960. Biological degradation of cellulose. Butterworth & Co., Ltd., London. 264 pp.

Goldblatt, L. A. 1969. Introduction. *In:* Goldblatt, L. A., Ed., Aflatoxin—scientific background, control and implications. Academic Press, New York. pp. 1–11.

Golumbic, C. 1965. Fungal spoilage in stored food crops. *In:* Wogan, G. N., Ed., Mycotoxins in foodstuffs. Massachusetts Institute of Technology Press, Cambridge, Mass. pp. 49–67.

Gray, W. D. 1959. The relation of fungi to human affairs. Holt, Rinehart & Winston, New York. 510 pp.

Gray, T. R. G. 1976. Survival of vegetative microbes in soil. Symp. Soc. Gen. Microbiol. **26**:327–364.

Greathouse, G. A., B. Fleer, and C. J. Wessel. 1954. Chemical and physical agents of deterioration. *In:* Greathouse, G. A., and C. J. Wessel, Eds., Deterioration of materials—causes and preventive techniques. Reinhold Publishing Co., Stamford, Conn. pp. 71–174.

Griffin, D. M. 1963. Soil physical factors and the ecology of fungi III. Activity of fungi in relatively dry soil. Trans. Brit. Mycol. Soc. **46**:373–377.

——. 1969. Soil water in the ecology of fungi. Ann. Rev. Phytopathol. **7**:289–310.

——. 1972. Ecology of soil fungi. Syracuse University Press, Syracuse. 193 pp.

Halver, J. E. 1969. Aflatoxicosis and trout hepatoma. *In:* Goldblatt, L. A., Ed., Aflatoxin—scientific background, control, and implications. Academic Press, New York. pp. 265–306.

Harley, J. L. 1960. The physiology of soil fungi. *In:* Parkinson, D., and J. S. Waid, Eds., The ecology of soil fungi: an international symposium. Liverpool University Press, Liverpool. pp. 265–276.

Henderson, M. E. K. 1960. Studies on the physiology of lignin decomposition by soil fungi. *In:* Parkinson, D., and J. S. Waid, Eds., The ecology of soil fungi: an international symposium. Liverpool University Press, Liverpool. pp. 286–296.

Hendey, N. I. 1964. Some observations on *Cladosporium resinae* as a fuel contaminant and its possible role in the corrosion of aluminum alloy fuel tanks. Trans. Brit. Mycol. Soc. **47**:467–475.

Hiscocks, E. S. 1965. The importance of molds in the deterioration of tropical foods and feedstuffs. *In:* Wogan, G. N., Ed., Mycotoxins in foodstuffs. Massachusetts Institute of Technology Press, Cambridge, Mass. pp. 15–26.

Hudson, H. J. 1968. The ecology of fungi on plant remains above the soil. New Phytologist Co., **67**: 837–874.

Hunt, G. M. 1954. Wood and wood products. *In:* Greathouse, G. A. and C. J. Wessel, Eds., Deterioration of materials—causes and preventive techniques. Reinhold Publishing Co., Stamford, Conn. pp. 308–354.

——, and G. A. Garratt. 1953. Wood preservation. McGraw-Hill Book Company, New York. 417 pp.

Elizabeth Moore-Landecker, *Fundamentals of the Fungi*, 2nd ed. (Englewood Cliffs, N.J.: Prentice-Hall, Inc., 1982), pp. 436–437.

1. Who wrote *Wood Preservation*? _____

2. What company published *Soil Fungi and Soil Fertility*? _____

3. When was Greathouse et al.'s work published? _____

4. What author would you consult if you wanted to know about prevention of materials deterioration? _____

5. Who is one of the authors on this list who wrote both a book and a journal article?

_____

6. How many pages did Brian's 1951 *Botanical Review* article occupy?

_____

7. Who edited the volume in which Burges' 1965 article was published?

_____

8. How long is the Gascoigne and Gascoigne text? _____

E. Look at the bibliography on page 141. Then match each word in column a with the author's evaluation in column b.

a	b
1. Blatt et al.	• detailed description and classification of carbonate rocks
2. H. Blatt	
3. Ham	• most comprehensive one-volume work on sedimentology
4. Pettijohn	• classic text in its third edition
5. Friedman and Sanders	• best book on carbonate sediments
6. Folk	• superb reference on sedimentary rocks
7. Bathurst	• best petrology book available
8. Pettijohn et al.	• excellent photomicrographs of terrigenous sedimentary rocks
	• somewhat of a companion volume to the present text

ADDITIONAL READING

BATHURST, R. G. C., 1975. *Carbonate Sediments and Their Diagenesis,* 2nd ed. Elsevier, Amsterdam, 660 p. (Chapters 1 and 2). This is probably the best single book currently available on carbonate sediments. Good discussions and illustrations on the various particle types that comprise carbonate sediments. The book is primarily concerned with modern and Holocene deposits.

BLATT, H., 1982. *Sedimentary Petrology.* W. H. Freeman, San Francisco, 555 p. Excellent treatment of the subject. The best book on petrology of sedimentary rocks currently available.

BLATT, H., MIDDLETON, G. V., AND MURRAY, R. C., 1980. *Origin of Sedimentary Rock,* 2nd ed. Prentice-Hall, Englewood Cliffs, N.J., 782 p. (Chapters 2, 8, 9, and 12–19). In some respects this book is a companion volume to the present book. The suggested chapters expand considerably on the subjects treated in the preceding chapter of this book.

FOLK, R. L., 1974. *Petrology of Sedimentary Rocks.* Hemphills, Austin, Tex., 170 p. Designed initially as a comprehensive syllabus for courses taught by Folk at the University of Texas, this book has evolved over 20 years into a superb reference on sediments and sedimentary rocks. It contains little on carbonates and some illustrations are difficult to interpret, but this book is a must for the serious student of sedimentology.

FRIEDMAN, G. M., AND SANDERS, J. E., 1978. *Principles of Sedimentology.* John Wiley, New York, 792 p. (Chapters 2, 3, 6, and 7). This book is perhaps the most comprehensive single volume on sedimentology available. It contains nearly 2000 references.

HAM, W. E. (ED.), 1962, *Classification of Carbonate Rocks.* Amer. Assoc. Petroleum Geologists, Mem. No. 1, Tulsa, Okla., 279 p. Most of the modern classifications of carbonate rocks are described and discussed in detail. Excellent photomicrographs of carbonates are presented.

PETTIJOHN, F. J., 1975. *Sedimentary Rocks,* 3rd ed. Harper & Row, New York, 628 p. (Chapters 2, 3,7, and 10). This third edition of Pettijohn's classic text is considerably expanded from earlier editions. Most of the discussion is descriptive.

PETTIJOHN, F. J., POTTER, P. E., AND SIEVER, R., 1972. *Sand and Sandstone.* Springer-Verlag, New York, 628 p. (Chapters 2, 3, 5, 6, and 10). Extensive discussion on petrography of sandstones and their diagenesis is presented. Excellent photomicrographs of terrigenous sedimentary rocks.

Richard A. David, Jr., *Depositional Systems: A Genetic Approach to Sedimentary Geology* (Englewood Cliffs, N.J.: Prentice-Hall, Inc., 1983), pp. 32–33.

Reading and Interpreting Charts, Tables, Diagrams, Graphs, Line Drawings, and Schematic Illustrations

Line Graphs

A comparison between two variables is often shown on a line graph. A line graph illustrates the relationship between a dependent and an independent variable, with one of them being plotted on a horizontal axis and one on a vertical axis.

The dependent variable changes as a result of changes in the independent variable. An example that illustrates the relationship between a dependent and an independent variable is the age and height of infants. The dependent variable is height because it depends on age, which increases regardless of any other factor. In other words, height increases as age increases.

example:

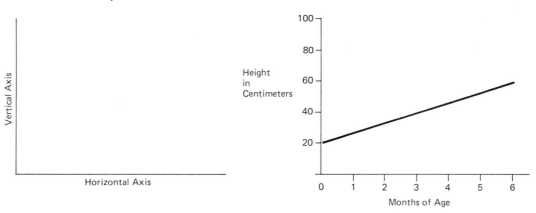

As with all graphs, charts, tables, diagrams, and the like, it is very important to read the title of the graph and any other explanations or captions and to be sure you know which is the dependent variable and which the independent.

Line Graphs

EXERCISES

F. Look at the line graph below. Then choose a or b to complete each of the statements that follow.

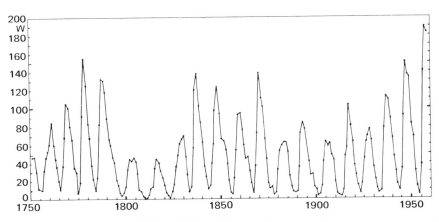

Sunspot numbers from 1750 to 1958 exhibit the 11-year cycle.

Donald H. Menzel, Fred L. Whipple, and Gerard de Vaucouleurs, *Survey of the Universe* (Englewood Cliffs, N.J.: Prentice-Hall, Inc., 1970), p. 155.

1. This graph describes _____ .
   a. sunspot frequency over a long period of time
   b. sunspot types over a long period of time

2. The period covered is _____ .
   a. 200 years
   b. 208 years

3. The horizontal axis shows _____ .
   a. year
   b. number

4. The vertical axis shows _____ .
   a. year
   b. number

5. The dependent variable is _____ .
   a. year
   b. number

6. The independent variable is _____ .
   a. year
   b. number

7. The number of sunspots _____.
   a. remains constant from year to year
   b. changes depending on the year

8. This graph primarily illustrates _____.
   a. sunspot periodicity
   b. the passage of time

G. Look at the line graph below. Then complete the paragraph that follows.

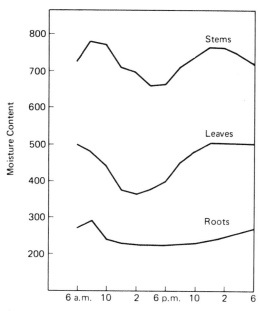

Figure 13-14. Fluctuation in the water content of leaves, roots, and stems of sunflower, on a clear, sunny day and the following night during the summer. The plant material was grown in the field, in the southeastern United States. Water content is expressed on a dry weight basis. (After Wilson et al., 1953; Figure 1.)

G. Ray Noggle and George J. Fritz, *Introductory Plant Physiology*, 2nd ed. (Englewood Cliffs, N.J.: Prentice-Hall, Inc., 1983), p. 408.

This graph compares (1) _____ content of three plant parts over

a (2) _____-hour period of time. The horizontal axis represents

(3) _____ and the vertical axis represents (4) _____ .

(5) _____ is dependent on (6) _____ .

The three plant parts in which moisture content measurements were compared are

(7) _____, (8) _____, and

(9) _____. The moisture content in these plant parts

(10) _____ with time. The measurements were taken in the

(11) _____ season. The weather during the day was

(12) _____ and (13) _____. At all times

the moisture content of the (14) _____ was higher than the moisture content of the other plant parts. At (15) _____ , the moisture content of the three plant parts was approximately equal to the measurement at the same time the next day. Leaf moisture content was lowest at

(16) _____ . (17) _____ moisture content was more constant over the 24-hour period than was that of the other two plant parts. (18) _____ content is (19) _____ during the daytime than it is at night. The plant studied was a

(20) _____ . From highest to lowest moisture content, plant parts can be ordered (21) _____ , (22) _____ ,

and then (23) _____ .

H. Look at the line graph below. Then answer the questions that follow.

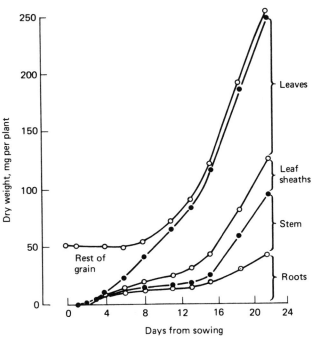

Figure 17-3. Dry weights of principal plant parts during early seedling growth. Constant environmental conditions at 20°C, 10 klux (After Williams, 1960; Figure 3.)

G. Ray Noggle and George J. Fritz, *Introductory Plant Physiology*, 2nd ed. (Englewood Cliffs, N.J.: Prentice-Hall, Inc., 1983), p. 520.

1. What does the horizontal axis show? _____

2. What does the vertical axis show? _____

3. Which is the independent variable? _____

4. In which plant part does weight grow at the fastest rate? _____

5. Which plant part starts out heaviest? _____

6. How heavy is the whole plant at 24 days? _____

7. Which plant part (not including the rest of the grain) weighs the most at 24 days?

   _____

8. How many plant parts (excluding the rest of the grain) are being compared?

   _____

Immune Responses

Macrophage destroying a foreign substance

All multicellular animals **possess** defense mechanisms that inactivate or eliminate **foreign** cells, destroy pathogenic microorganisms and their products, remove **worn out** or damaged cells, and destroy abnormal or mutant (cancer) cells that arise in the body. This defense system **resides** in the body fluids. Phylogenetically, phagocytosis is the most ancient mechanism for dealing with foreign materials, and this phenomenon remains a **cornerstone** of immunity from the protozoans to the most advanced mammals. Encapsulation is a related process in which masses too large for engulfment **are walled off** or isolated by large numbers of phagocytes. In addition, the vascular fluids of the more highly organized invertebrates with circulatory systems contain humoral factors (agglutinins) that inactivate foreign materials. These three mechanisms (phagocytosis, encapsulation, and the action of agglutinins) are universal, relatively non-

vascular: related to the circulatory system

1

From William S. Hoar, *General and Comparative Physiology*, 3rd ed. (Englewood Cliffs, N.J.: Prentice-Hall, Inc., 1983), pp. 457–459.

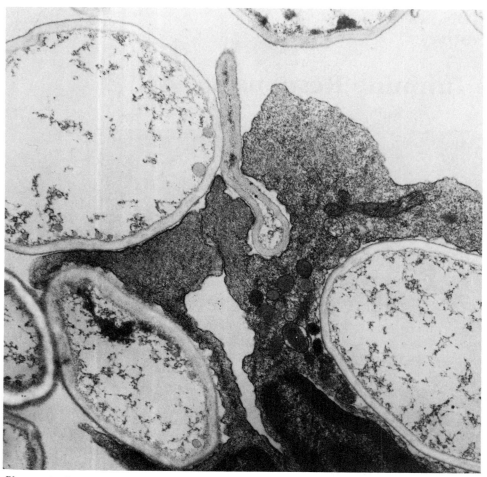

Phagocytosis
S. Hoffstem, N.Y.U., Photo Researchers, Inc.

specific in nature, and based on an ability to recognize "self" and "nonself." The production of highly specific antibodies in vertebrate animals adds a further dimension to the immune responses. Antibodies may be circulating plasma proteins (humoral) or associated directly with sensitized lymphocytes (cell-mediated). This system of adaptive immunity differs from the immune defenses of invertebrates in its specificity and its acquired nature; there is an immunologic memory as well as the recognition of self and nonself.

plasma: blood minus the cells and platelets

Phagocytosis and Encapsulation

erythrocytes: red blood cells

If foreign cells such as human erythrocytes are injected into the mesoglea of a sponge, numerous ameboid cells will **cluster** to engulf them or surround and encapsulate masses of them. The phagocytes or encapsulated masses then **migrate** into the excurrent canals and are excreted. These three processes (phagocytosis, encapsulation, transport to the exterior) are universal among the multicellular animals; they depend on a simple recognition of self and nonself. Similar capacities of recognition are **evident** in tissue graft experiments where a very fine discrimination is evident even in the most primitive invertebrates. Thus, in the colonial sponge *Callyspongia diffusa*, isografts (tissues from the same individual or colony) **fuse** compatibly but allografts (tissues of the same species but different genotypes) are invariably incompatible (Hildemann and Johnson, 1979).

The least specialized invertebrates (Porifera, Cnidaria) depend on **scattered** ameboid cells. The evolution of invertebrates with complex organ systems and a circulation of body fluids is associated with much more highly organized mechanisms of defense. This phylogeny involves the development of (1) several types of phagocytic cell, (2) an ability to respond to foreign or useless materials by increased phagocyte **proliferation**, and (3) the presence of special lymphogenous or phagocytic organs where the proliferation of phagocytes occurs. Special sites of phagocyte proliferation have been described in many animals from the annelids to the vertebrates (Manning and Turner, 1976); some of the most highly organized of these "lymphoid tissues" occur in the cephalopods whose hematopoietic or blood-forming centers are referred to as "white bodies" and "branchial spleens." The invertebrate immune system responds to extra demands by intense proliferation of phagocytes; for example, marine polychaetes at the end of the breeding season show greatly increased numbers of phagocytes when large numbers of unshed eggs are being removed, as do many arthropods at the time of the molt (Gardiner, 1972). It must be emphasized, however, that the lymphogenous glands or "lymphoid tissues" of invertebrates are *not* **homologous** with the lymph glands of vertebrates.

Invertebrate Hemagglutinins

Several humoral factors concerned with the immune response have been described in annelids and all more advanced stages in phylogeny (Manning and Turner, 1976). Many of these are naturally occurring hemagglutinins. Thus, the blood cells of the sipunculid worm *Dendrostomum* contain factors that react with human anti-A and anti-B serum; the serum of the spiny lobster *Palinurus* contains at least 10 factors that will agglutinate the sperm or erythrocytes of various animals; the Atlantic lobster has a factor in its serum which **clumps** the red cells of the herring; seminal fluids of many animals contain natural antibodies which clump sperm or cells of other species. These examples could be multiplied; **the literature** on blood group reactive substances is extensive and has been carefully reviewed (Boyden, 1964; Manning and Turner, 1976). These reactions depend on highly specific proteins (whose syntheses are genetically controlled. In the Crustacea, the agglutinins are hemolymph proteins that are not associated with hemocyanin (Tyler and Scheer, 1945; Schapiro, 1975; Manning and Turner, 1976). In some cases these interactions are probably **fortuitous** and of no particular biological significance; the interactions between sipunculid blood cells and human blood sera seem to be of this sort. In other cases these reactions are highly important to the species; the chemicals that control the interactions between eggs and sperm are in this class (Raven, 1966; Cooper and Brown, 1972).

Adaptive Immunity

Jawed vertebrates have the ability to form specific antibodies in response to many foreign substances. This capacity depends on the presence of plasma cells and lymphocytes that **elaborate** a special group of plasma proteins, the γ-globulins capable of reacting specifically with the foreign substance or antigen. Organisms capable of an adaptive immunity must be able to distinguish "self" from "nonself" and possess an "immunologic memory." Adaptive immunity differs from the primitive defense mechanisms of invertebrates in its characteristic specificity and its acquired nature. The phylogeny of adaptive or acquired immunity parallels the evolution of the vertebrate lymphoid tissues.

Although immune responses **are** usually **evoked** by foreign proteins, they may develop with other large molecules (mol wt 10,000 or more) like some of the polysaccharides. The antigenic material is often a part of foreign cells or bacteria, but it may be a protein in solution. A primary response **is induced** by the first injection. This normally passes unnoticed, but at the tissue level it promotes the elaboration of antibodies. A second exposure produces a violent reaction between antibody and antigen with a variety of distressing symptoms and sometimes death. The antibody molecules seem to act as bridges between the foreign particles, linking them together in large clumps which may later dissolve or be phagocytized. These reactions are markedly specific. As yet it is not clearly understood how an antigen stimulates cells to elaborate antibodies. Several theories have been proposed, and details may be found in textbooks and monographs on immunology.

4

5

6

Vocabulary

to possess (verb)

to have

All multicellular animals **possess** defense mechanisms that inactivate or eliminate foreign cells, destroy pathogenic microorganisms and their products, remove worn out or damaged cells, and destroy abnormal or mutant (cancer) cells that arise in the body.

foreign (adjective)

not belonging; in an abnormal place

All multicellular animals possess defense mechanisms that inactivate or eliminate **foreign** cells, destroy pathogenic microorganisms and their products, remove worn out or damaged cells, and destroy abnormal or mutant (cancer) cells that arise in the body.

worn out (adjective)

used up; old and useless

All multicellular animals possess defense mechanisms that inactivate or eliminate foreign cells, destroy pathogenic microorganisms and their products, remove **worn out** or damaged cells, and destroy abnormal or mutant (cancer) cells that arise in the body.

to reside (verb)

to be situated; to exist

This defense system **resides** in the body fluids.

cornerstone (noun)

basic, fundamental, distinguishing feature

Phylogenetically, phagocytosis is the most ancient mechanism for dealing with foreign materials, and this phenomenon remains a **cornerstone** of immunity from the protozoans to the most advanced mammals.

to wall off (verb)

to build a wall around (something) in order to isolate it.

Encapsulation is a related process in which masses too large for engulfment **are walled off** or isolated by large numbers of phagocytes.

to cluster (verb)

to form a group; to gather together

If foreign cells such as human erythrocytes are injected into the mesoglea of a sponge, numerous ameboid cells **will cluster** to engulf them or surround and encapsulate masses of them.

to migrate (verb)

to travel

The phagocytes or encapsulated masses then **migrate** into the excurrent canals and are excreted.

evident (adjective)

obvious; visible; basic

Similar capacities of recognition are **evident** in tissue graft experiments where a very fine discrimination is evident even in the most primitive invertebrates.

to fuse (verb)

to become united, to mix permanently as if by heating together

Thus, in the colonial sponge *Callyspongia diffusa*, isografts (tissues from the same individual or colony) **fuse** compatibly but allografts (tissues of the same species but different genotypes) are invariably incompatible (Hildemann and Johnson, 1979).

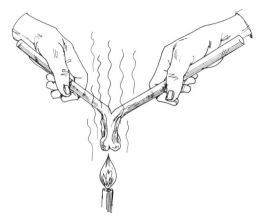

to scatter (verb)

to disperse; to put in various places; to separate widely

The least specialized invertebrates depend on **scattered** ameboid cells.

proliferation (noun)

growth; increase in number; reproduction

This phylogeny involves the development of (1) several types of phagocytic cell, (2) an ability to respond to foreign or useless materials by increased phagocyte **proliferation**, and (3) the presence of special lymphogenous or phagocytic organs where the proliferation of phagocytes occurs.

homologous (adjective)

structurally or functionally equivalent

It must be emphasized, however, that the lymphogenous glands or "lymphoid tissues" of invertebrates are *not* **homologous** with the lymph glands of vertebrates.

to clump (verb)

to draw together; to stick together, doing medical damage

. . . [T]he Atlantic lobster has a factor in its serum which **clumps** the red cells of the herring; seminal fluids of many animals contain natural antibodies which clump sperm or cells of other species.

(the) literature (noun)

(the) body of written recent scientific articles and books on a specific topic

The examples could be multiplied; **the literature** on blood group reactive substances is extensive and has been carefully reviewed (Boyden, 1964; Manning and Turner, 1976).

fortuitous (adjective)

by chance; random; unplanned or accidental

In some cases these interactions are probably **fortuitous** and of no particular biological significance; the interactions between sipunculid blood cells and human blood sera seem to be of this sort.

to elaborate (verb)

to develop; to produce (a thing)

This capacity depends on the presence of plasma cells and lymphocytes that **elaborate** a special group of plasma proteins, the γ-globulins capable of reacting specifically with the foreign substance or antigen.

to evoke (verb)

to cause; to produce (an action)

Although immune responses **are** usually **evoked** by foreign proteins, they may develop with other large molecules (mol wt 10,000 or more) like some of the polysaccharides.

to induce (verb)

> to encourage to occur; to cause; to produce

> A primary response **is induced** by the first injection.

Vocabulary Exercises

A. Complete the following statements with words from the list.

scatter	homologous	cornerstone
proliferation	worn out	possess
fused	fortuitious	walled off
		literature

1. The cell membrane of a protozoan is _____ to the skin in a higher organism.

2. In some ways the words *cluster* and _____ are antonyms.

3. A study of the recent _____ indicates a shift in emphasis from earthquake prediction to earthquake prevention.

4. A _____ of current thinking in hypertension management is sodium reduction.

Agglutinated blood
Carolina Biological Supply

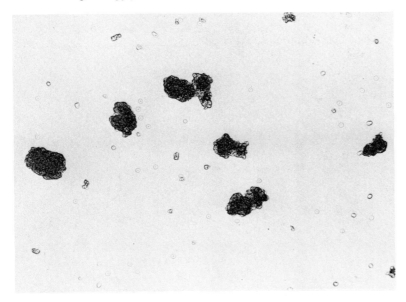

5. There has been a recent _____ of noninvasive diagnostic techniques.

6. When a gear is _____ it must be replaced.

7. Sharks appear to _____ some anticancer agent in their blood.

8. In the heat of some boilers, temperatures get so high that metals can be

_____ .

9. It appears that sunspot periodicity is in no way _____ .

10. Rooms in which X-rays or radioactive materials are used should be

_____ .

B. Choose the best response to complete each numbered statement.

1. One word that does not mean "to produce" is _____ .
   a. to elaborate
   b. to reside
   c. to induce
   d. to evoke

2. An antigen can cause the red blood cells to _____ and can therefore be very damaging.
   a. scatter
   b. clump
   c. migrate
   d. elaborate

3. Currently several new plastic batteries have been _____ and are undergoing testing.
   a. resided
   b. fused
   c. evoked
   d. elaborated

4. It is _____ that the new propfan represents an exciting development in aircraft engines.
   a. evident
   b. homologous
   c. fortuitous
   d. foreign

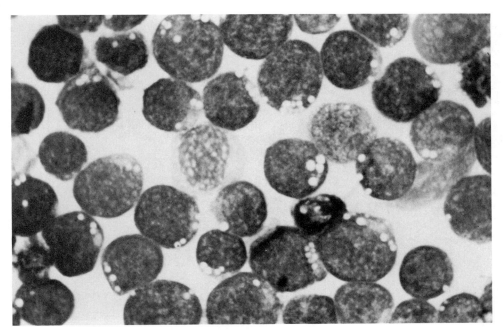

B-cells: lymphocytes of the immune system, which secrete antibodies
NCI/Science Source, Photo Researchers, Inc.

5. Cancer cells can _____ throughout the body and cause new or secondary tumors.
   a. clump
   b. possess
   c. migrate
   d. induce

6. Getting a _____ substance in the eye can be very painful.
   a. foreign
   b. fortuitous
   c. evident
   d. homologous

7. Many animals _____ together for defense of the group as a whole.
   a. elaborate
   b. scatter
   c. fuse
   d. cluster

Analysis of monoclonal antibodies in a cancer research laboratory
NCI/Science Source, Photo Researchers, Inc.

8. Some antigens _____ an immediate response.
   a. evoke
   b. reside
   c. clump
   d. elaborate

9. It is thought that many long-term climate changes may have been

   _____ by sunspot activity.
   a. possessed
   b. induced
   c. walled off
   d. worn out

Comprehension

I. Meaning

EXERCISE

C. Respond T if the statement is true or F if the statement is false.

_____ 1. The reading selection is about the mechanism of self protection against noxious agents within the body.

_____ 2. The immune system can eliminate foreign cells.

_____ 3. Cancer cells are mutant cells.

_____ 4. The immune system is in the solid parts of the body.

_____ 5. Phagocytosis is a mechanism that exists only in higher animals.

_____ 6. Protozoans possess the mechanism of phagocytosis.

_____ 7. *To isolate* (¶ 1) is similar to *to wall off.*

_____ 8. Encapsulation and phagocytosis are two related immune mechanisms.

_____ 9. Phagocytes can both engulf and wall off pathogens.

_____ 10. Agglutinins can be found in the most primitive animals.

_____ 11. The ability to recognize self from nonself is the cornerstone of the immune system.

_____ 12. Phagocytosis, encapsulation, and agglutinin activity are processes directed against specific foreign materials.

_____ 13. Antibody production is universal throughout the animal kingdom.

_____ 14. Two kinds of antibodies are humoral and cell-mediated.

_____ 15. Adaptive immunity cannot be acquired.

_____ 16. The mesoglea is made up of cells foreign to the sponge.

_____ 17. The ameboid cells of the sponge engulf foreign cells.

_____ 18. The sponge possesses excurrent canals.

_____ 19. The reason allografts don't work in the colonial sponge is that the various members of the colony recognize material that is genetically dissimilar.

_____ 20. If two things are compatible, they can exist together harmoniously.

_____ 21. In an isograft the host sponge recognizes the graft as nonself.

_____ 22. Cephalopods produce a large number of phagocytes.

_____ 23. *Hematopoietic* means "white bodies."

_____ 24. The proliferation of phagocytes that occurs in invertebrates is homologous to the lymph glands of vertebrates.

_____ 25. There are substances in worm and arthropod blood that form part of their immune systems.

_____ 26. The fact that different species cannot cross-breed is probably due to the immune system.

_____ 27. Boyden reported on blood group reactive substances in 1976.

_____ 28. All blood group reactions are of crucial importance to the survival of the species possessing them.

_____ 29. We can presume that vertebrates without jaws do not have systems of adaptive immunity.

_____ 30. An antigen is a foreign substance.

_____ 31. Adaptive immunity is nonspecific and inborn.

_____ 32. In paragraph 6, *injection* means placement within the body by use of a needle.

_____ 33. After the first exposure to certain antigens, antibodies are formed in adaptive immunity.

_____ 34. Antibodies clump the foreign particles as a step in eliminating them.

_____ 35. The mechanism of antibody elaboration is well understood.

II. Reference

EXERCISE

D. Choose a or b to indicate the reference for the italicized word or phrase in each of the following statements taken from the reading on pages 147-150. Paragraph numbers are indicated.

1. All multicellular animals possess defense mechanisms that inactivate or eliminate foreign cells, destroy pathogenic microorganisms and *their* products, remove worn out or damaged cells, and destroy abnormal or mutant (cancer) cells that arise in the body. (¶ 1)
   a. of pathogenic microorganisms
   b. of defense mechanisms

2. Phylogenetically, phagocytosis is the most ancient mechanism for dealing with foreign materials, and *this phenomenon* remains a cornerstone of immunity from the protozoans to the most advanced mammals. (¶ 1)
   a. foreign materials
   b. phagocytosis

3. *These three mechanisms* (phagocytosis, encapsulation, and the action of agglutinins) are universal, relatively nonspecific in nature, and based on an ability to recognize "self" and "nonself." (¶ 1)
   a. universal, relatively nonspecific, and recognizable
   b. phagocytosis, encapsulation, and the action of agglutinins

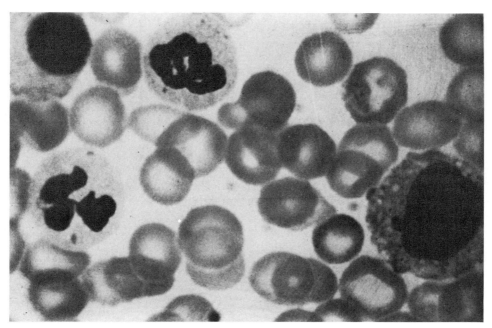

Normal white blood cell monocytes (stained)
National Institutes of Health

4. If foreign cells such as human erythrocytes are injected into the mesoglea of a sponge, numerous ameboid cells will cluster to engulf them or surround and encapsulate *masses of them.* (¶ 2)
   a. ameboid cells
   b. human erythrocytes

5. These three processes (phagocytosis, encapsulation, transport to the exterior) are universal among the multicellular animals; *they* depend on a simple recognition of self and nonself. (¶ 2)
   a. multicellular animals
   b. phagocytosis, encapsulation, transport to the exterior

6. *This phylogeny* involves the development of (1) several types of phagocytic cell, (2) an ability to respond to foreign or useless materials by increased phagocyte proliferation, and (3) the presence of special lymphogenous or phagocytic organs where the proliferation of phagocytes occurs. (¶ 3)
   a. invertebrates with complex organ systems
   b. highly organized mechanisms of defense

7. Many of *these* are naturally occurring hemagglutinins. (¶ 4)
    a. humoral factors
    b. annelids

8. *These examples* could be multiplied. (¶ 4)
    a. of naturally occurring hemagglutinins
    b. of seminal fluids

9. In some cases *these interactions* are probably fortuitous and of no particular bio-
    logical significance. . . . (¶ 4)
    a. between proteins in the blood of various species
    b. between Tyler and Scheer, Schapiro, and Manning and Turner

10. In other cases these reactions are highly important to the species; the chemicals
    that control the interactions between eggs and sperm are in *this class*. (¶ 4)
    a. those fortuitious and of no particular biological significance
    b. those important to the species

11. *This capacity* depends on the presence of plasma cells and lymphocytes that elab-
    orate a special group of plasma proteins, the γ-globulins capable of reacting specifi-
    cally with the foreign substance or antigen. (¶ 5)
    a. to form specific antibodies
    b. to depend on plasma cells

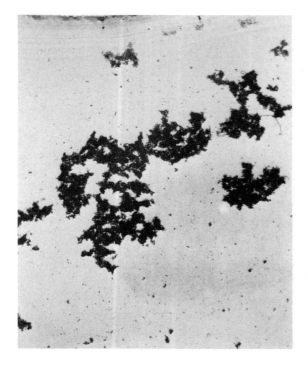

*Antibodies in blood serum
(clumped)*
Martin M. Rotker, Taurus Photos

12. Adaptive immunity differs from the primitive defense mechanisms of the inverte-brates in *its* characteristic specificity and *its* acquired nature. (¶ 5)
    a. of primitive defense mechanisms
    b. of adaptive immunity

13. Although immune responses are usually evoked by foreign proteins, *they* may develop with other large molecules (mol wt 10,000 or more) like some of the polysaccharides. (¶ 6)
    a. foreign proteins
    b. immune responses

14. The antigenic material is often a part of foreign cells or bacteria, but *it* may be a protein in solution (¶ 6)
    a. a part of foreign cells or bacteria
    b. the antigenic material

15. *This* normally passes unnoticed, but at the tissue level it promotes the elaboration of antibodies. (¶ 6)
    a. primary response
    b. the first injection

16. The antibody molecules seem to act as bridges between the foreign particles, link-ing *them* together in large clumps which may later dissolve or be phagocytized. (¶ 6)
    a. the foreign particles
    b. the antibody molecules

III. Syntax: Adjective Clauses and Phrases

EXERCISE

E. Write the antecedent for each of the following adjective clauses and phrases taken from the reading on pages 147–150. Paragraph numbers are indicated.

1. . . . that inactivate or eliminate foreign cells . . . (¶ 1) _____

2. . . . [that] destroy pathogenic microorganisms and their products . . . (¶ 1)

    _____

3. . . . [that] remove worn out or damaged cells . . . (¶ 1) _____

4. . . . [that] destroy abnormal or mutant (cancer) cells . . . (¶ 1)

    _____

5. . . . that arise in the body. (¶ 1) _____

6. . . . in which masses too large for engulfment are walled off or isolated by large numbers of phagocytes. (¶ 1) _____

7. . . . that inactivate foreign materials. (¶ 1) _____

8. . . . whose hematopoietic or blood-forming centers are referred to as "white bodies" and "branchial spleens." (¶ 3) _____

9. . . . concerned with the immune response . . . (¶ 4) _____

10. . . . that react with human anti-A and anti-B serum . . . (¶ 4)

_____

11. . . . which clumps the red cells of the herring . . . (¶ 4) _____

12. . . . which clump sperm or cells of other species. (¶ 4) _____

13. . . . whose syntheses are genetically controlled. (¶ 4) _____

14. . . . that are not associated with hemocyanin . . . (¶ 4) _____

15. . . . that control the interactions . . . (¶ 4) _____

16. . . . that elaborate a special group of plasma proteins . . . (¶ 5)

_____

17. . . . capable of reacting specifically with the foreign substance or antigen. (¶ 5)

_____

18. . . . capable of an adaptive immunity . . . (¶ 5) _____

19. . . . which may later dissolve or be phagocytized (¶ 6) _____

COMPREHENSION SKILL INDEX

Prediction: Outline Format

The skeleton of a good textbook or some part of that book is an *outline*. An outline is simply an organizational framework for ideas. Often the outline hierarchy is evident from chapter heads and subheads.

The reading selection in this lesson, although a small excerpt from a large work, is a good example of the simplest form of outline arrangement.

example: Immune Responses (head)

1. Phagocytosis and encapsulation (subhead)
2. Invertebrate hemagglutinins (subhead)
3. Adaptive immunity (subhead)

Skimming these pages and looking only at the heads and subheads will give you a very good idea of what information will be contained in each section. In addition, even if you know nothing about immune responses, the outline followed by the author indicates to you that three types of immune responses are phagocytosis and encapsulation, hemagglutinins, and adaptive immunity.

IV. Prediction: Outline Format

EXERCISES

F. Using logic and your knowledge of the outline followed by the author of the reading selection in this lesson, put the following sentences taken from it in order by numbering them in the space provided.

_____ The invertebrate immune system responds to extra demands by intense proliferation of phagocytes; for example, marine polychaetes at the end of the breeding season show greatly increased numbers of phagocytes when large numbers of unshed eggs are being removed, as do many arthropods at the time of the molt.

_____ These three mechanisms (phagocytosis, encapsulation, and the action of agglutinins) are universal, relatively nonspecific in nature, and based on an ability to recognize "self" and "nonself."

_____ Adaptive immunity differs from the primitive defense mechanisms of invertebrates in its characteristic specificity and its acquired nature.

_____ The serum of the spiny lobster *Palinurus* contains at least 10 factors that will agglutinate the sperm or erythrocytes of various animals.

G. Look at the following outline of Lesson Two of this text. Then make your own outline of Lesson Nine on page 166.

Lesson Two
  Materials
    Textbook Features
      Title Page
      Copyright Page
      Table of Contents
    Reading and Interpreting Charts, Tables, Diagrams, Graphs, Line Drawings, and Schematic Illustrations
      Tables
      Charts

_____

_____

_____

_____

_____

_____

_____

_____

_____

_____

LESSON TEN
Materials

Textbook Features

Footnotes

Many textbooks and almost all journal articles include footnotes or notes. The use of a footnote is obligatory when an author quotes another writer directly or restates or refers to an idea or conclusion that comes from another author.

Although these notes are commonly referred to as *footnotes* (because they are often located at the "foot" or bottom of the page on which the original reference was made), they can be found in several different places: at the bottom of the page, at the end of the article or chapter, or at the end of the book itself, in the back matter. More and more, however, notes are being used within the text itself. This is especially true of scientific and technical writing.

examples:

(*within the text itself, when a reference list or bibliography follows*)

It is has been reported that the elusive anti-cancer factor within shark blood may be a sodium compound (Tiburon, 1977, 36).

(*at the bottom of the page or at the end of the book, when there is no reference list or bibliography included*)

It has been reported that the elusive anti-cancer factor within shark blood may be a sodium compound.[1]

[1] Charles Carcharia Tiburon. 1987. *Physiology of the Vertebrates* (Greenwich, Conn.: Lucas Press), 36.

Sometimes you will see the shortened form at the bottom of the page when a reference list is included. The more citations the author uses, the more likely he or she is to use the shortened form right on the page of the reference (either within the text or at the bottom of the page). When there are very few footnotes, it makes more sense to give the full bibliographic information immediately, close to the reference.

Often an author annotates the footnotes with comments about what was said in the original source or with an evaluation or general description of the source as a whole.

examples:

SIMPLE:

[2] Carla M. Rosenberg. 1985. *The Chemistry and Physics of Cooking* (New York: Bluestone Publishing Company), 144.

ANNOTATED:

[2] Carla M. Rosenberg. 1985. *The Chemistry and Physics of Cooking* (New York: Bluestone Publishing Company), 144. Rosenberg includes many experiments that illustrate basic concepts in physics and chemistry. These experiments may be carried out in the kitchen of the average home, with no unusual equipment.

When footnotes are extensive, authors often use the terms *ibid.* and *op. cit.* in order to save space. *Ibid.* is an abbreviation of the Latin *ibidem*, meaning "in the same place." It is used to avoid repeating all the bibliographic information listed in the immediately preceding footnote.

example:

[3] Elizabeth Potter. 1966. *Clinical Management of the Lifelong Diabetic* (Long Beach, N.J.: Binghamton Green, Inc.), pp. 88–91.

[4] *Ibid.*, 97.

Op. cit. is an abbreviation of the Latin *opere citato*, meaning "in the work cited." It is used to avoid repeating full bibliographic information for a book previously (but not immediately before) cited in the list of footnotes.

example:

[5] John L. Martínez. 1984. *Piston Engine Maintenance and Repair* (San Diego, California: Ball Publishing Company), 22.

[6] Elton Hakim. 1984. *Propfan Technology* (Tucson, Ariz.: Jones and Jones), 55.

[7] Martínez, *op. cit.*, 10.

    You will find many variants of footnote style, but their differences are not important to you as a reader. What is important is that you understand the various bits of information included in them so that you may understand where an idea originated or by whom particular research was performed or reported. The footnote, either alone or in combination with a bibliography and/or reference list, will help you find the original sources if you are interested in doing so.

Footnotes

EXERCISE

A. Look at the footnotes below. Then respond T if the statements that follow are true or F if they are false.

[1] Guzmán, 766.

[2] Crown (1988), 201.

[3] Picar and Picar, 21. The authors' point of view is considered unorthodox by traditional paleontologists.

[4] Guzmán. *op. cit.*, 36–42.

[5] *Ibid.*, xiv.

[6] Robinson et al., 1958, 66.

[7] Robinson, 72.

[8] *Ibid.*, 56.

_____ 1. There is a bibliography elsewhere in the book where these footnotes are found.

_____ 2. Crown wrote only one work.

_____ 3. This is not an annotated list.

_____ 4. The eighth note refers to Robinson et al.'s 1958 work.

_____ 5. Guzmán's work is cited three times in this list.

_____ 6. Notes 6 and 7 refer to the same work.

_____ 7. Note 4 refers to the same work as note 1.

The Internal Structure of Textbooks

As we saw in Lesson Nine, most textbooks are organized in outline form. Since our purpose here is not writing, but reading and textbook use, we will not practice making outlines. However, a general understanding of the outline format is extremely helpful in our using of published material.

Remember that an outline is a format for grouping related materials and ideas and for organizing them in a hierarchy of importance. When you perceive the outline an author has used, you can analyze the relationship of his or her ideas to one another and understand the relative importance of the various concepts presented in the work.

Most textbooks as a whole are organized in outline and most chapters or lessons within them use the outline format too.

example:

Title of Book

I. Part
   A. Chapter
      1. Section
      2. Section
      3. Section
   B. Chapter
      1. Section
      2. Section
   C. Chapter
      1. Section
      2. Section

II. Part
   A. Chapter
      1. Section
      2. Section
   B. Chapter
      1. Section
      2. Section
      3. Section
      4. Section

III. Part
    A. Chapter
       1. Section
       2. Section
    B. Chapter

The example above shows the internal structure of a hypothetical textbook as a whole. You can see that the book has three major parts, which in turn are divided into chapters. Most of the chapters are then divided into sections. Note that in Lesson Nine we saw that chapters and lessons are also usually organized in outline format.

The Internal Structure of Textbooks

EXERCISE

B. Show the general internal structure of one of your textbooks here. Show only the major general outline.

_____

_____

_____

_____

_____

_____

_____

_____

_____

_____

_____

_____

_____

_____

_____

_____

_____

_____

Understanding Textbook Typography

Most textbooks are designed in such a way that you can immediately see the organization of subject matter simply by skimming the heads within each chapter. (The heads are the titles of each section, part, or other division of a book). Although these guidelines are not infallible, you can usually guess the relative importance (and therefore the relationship) of various subsections of each larger section if you understand the conventions of basic typographic design.

1. The larger the type size of the head, the more important the material that follows.
2. Heads printed entirely in capital letters indicate more important material than do heads in uppercase and lowercase letters.
3. A combination of uppercase and lowercase letters indicates more importance than all lowercase letters.
4. Boldface type indicates greater importance than lightface.
5. Heads that appear a line above the material they introduce indicate greater importance than heads run in on the same line with the material they introduce.

> *examples:* (corresponding to the five conventions above) Below we can see from the typography alone that "Ancient Beginnings" introduces material subordinate to "The Origins of the Computer." We may assume, furthermore, that "Ancient Beginnings" will introduce material that will be about "The Origins of the Computer."

1. The Origins of the Computer
   Ancient Beginnings
2. THE ORIGINS OF THE COMPUTER
   Ancient Beginnings

3. The Origins of the Computer
ancient beginnings

4. **THE ORIGINS OF THE COMPUTER**
ANCIENT BEGINNINGS

5. The Origins of the Computer
Ancient Beginnings _____ (text) _____

_____

Understanding Textbook Typography

EXERCISES

C. Put the following heads (indicating the classification of humans on the evolutionary scale) in descending hierarchical order, based on the typography.

Mammalia

Animalia

Primates

Homo

CHORDATA

sapiens

Homididae

1. (kingdom) _____
2. (phylum) _____
3. (class) _____
4. (order) _____
5. (family) _____
6. (genus) _____
7. (species) _____

D. List the heads in one chapter of one of your textbooks. Place the most important heads farthest to the left. List the next parallel group farther to the right. Place the most subordinate heads farthest to the right. See how skimming these can tell you about the organization of the material and even give you a good idea of the content itself. (If there are more than three levels of heads, use only the three most important ones.)

most important heads

_____

_____

_____

_____

_____

_____

_____

_____

_____

next most important

_____

_____

_____

_____

_____

_____

_____

_____

_____

_____

_____

_____

_____

_____

most subordinate

_____

_____

_____

_____

_____

_____

_____

_____

_____

_____

_____

_____

_____

_____

_____

Reading and Interpreting Charts, Tables, Diagrams, Graphs, Line Drawings, and Schematic Illustrations

Line Drawings and Schematic Illustrations

Scientific and technical books make heavy use of line drawings and schematic illustrations. These visuals are specially drawn to illustrate difficult concepts and processes or to show how to do something or how something works. These last two uses are most common in technical books and manuals.

Authors rely on these drawings because they are usually clearer than photographs in that they are drawn exactly to specifications and show exactly what the author wants to show. In addition, they do not contain any extraneous information that would dilute the information the author wants to convey.

There are several important features of these drawings. Most illustrations in large textbooks are designated with a *figure number and a title.* In addition, parts of these illustrations often have *labels* explaining what that specific part pictures. Further, lines or arrows may connect smaller parts of these illustrations with additional labels.

We are discussing line drawings and schematic illustrations together here, although technical differences between the two do exist. The term *schematic illustration* is most often used to describe a line drawing that is simplified to an unrealistic degree in order to make something especially understandable. A drawing of a living cell, for example, frequently does not really look like a cell, but rather is symbolic of the cell in that an example of each cell component is shown.

example:

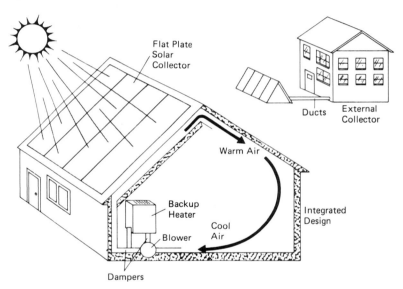

Flat-plate collector used in heating a home

Bernard S. Nebel, *Environmental Science: The Way the World Works* (Englewood Cliffs, N.J.: Prentice-Hall, Inc., 1981), p. 603.

It would be impossible to show this system in a photograph, because the side of the house could not be cut away to show it. Furthermore, a photograph would contain so much additional content that the illustration of the heating system would get lost.

Note the title of the illustration is "Flat-plate collector used in heating a home," the labels are "Integrated Design," and "External Collector," and the callouts are "Flat Plate Solar Collector," "Warm Air," "Backup Heater," "Blower," "Dampers," "Cool Air," and "Ducts."

Line Drawings and Schematic Illustrations

EXERCISES

E. Look at the illustration below. Then respond T if the statements are true or F if they are false.

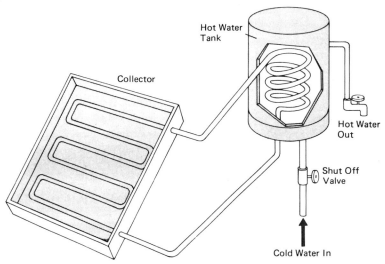

Flat-plate collector used for heating water

Bernard S. Nebel, *Environmental Science: The Way the World Works* (Englewood Cliffs, N.J.: Prentice-Hall, Inc., 1981), p. 603.

_____ 1. This illustration shows electrical circuitry.

_____ 2. This illustration shows a water heating system.

_____ 3. The device is made up of two main parts.

_____ 4. The illustration has no general label.

_____ 5. There are six callouts to the various parts of the system.

_____ 6. The system cannot be shut off.

_____ 7. Hot water is cooled in this system.

_____ 8. Hot water results from this system.

F. Look at the following illustration and then choose the correct response to answer each question.

	Auxin	Gibberellin	Cytokinin	Abscisic acid
Shoot tip	+ + +	+ + +	+ + +	+
Young leaves	+ + +	+ + +	+ + +	+
Elongating stem	+ +	+ +	+ + +	+
Lateral buds	+	+ +	+	+ +
Flowers and fruits	+	+	+ +	+
Developing seeds	+	+ + +	+ +	+ +
Mature leaves	+	+	+	+ + +
Lateral shoot	+ + +	+ +	+ +	+
Mature stem	+	+	+	+
Root	+	+	+	+
Root tip	+	+ +	+ + +	+

Figure 17-12. Relative concentrations of some plant growth substances in various parts of the plant. +++ high concentration, ++ medium concentration, + low concentration.

G. Ray Noggle and George J. Fritz, *Introductory Plant Physiology*, 2nd ed. (Englewood Cliffs, N.J.: Prentice-Hall, Inc., 1983), p. 535.

1. What is the subject of this illustration?
    a. which plant parts grow faster
    b. the quantities of certain substances in certain plant parts

2. What kind of plant is this?
    a. four kinds: auxin, gibberellin, cytokinin, abscisic acid
    b. any kind of plant

3. How much of the plant does the illustration show?
    a. an example of all plant parts
    b. everything except the root

4. From where does a lateral shoot arise?
    a. from the joint between the mature stem and a mature leaf
    b. from the shoot tip

5. Which two plant parts are very closely physically associated?
    a. flowers and fruits
    b. roots and mature leaves

6. What are auxin, gibberellin, cytokinin, and abscisic acid?
    a. various plant parts
    b. various plant growth substances

7. What is the indicator symbol for high concentration?
    a. +
    b. +++

8. Which of the following pairs of plant parts have the same concentration of all substances?
    a. young leaves and shoot tip
    b. shoot tip and root tip

9. Which two plant parts have the lowest concentrations of all substances?
    a. auxin and abscisic acid
    b. mature stem and root

10. Which plant part has a lower concentration of cytokinin?
    a. mature stem
    b. flowers and fruits

11. Which plant parts contain the highest concentrations of the growth substances?
    a. the younger parts
    b. the older parts

G. Look at the illustration below and then choose the correct response to complete the statements that follow.

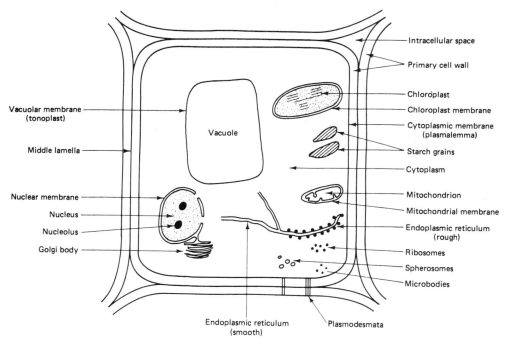

Figure 2-2 Generalized plant cell.

G. Ray Noggle and George J. Fritz, *Introductory Plant Physiology*, 2nd ed. (Englewood Cliffs, N.J.: Prentice-Hall, Inc., 1983), p. 12.

1. This is a drawing of a _____ .
   a. vacuole
   b. plant cell

2. It is _____ .
   a. absolutely realistic
   b. schematic

3. The cell is surrounded by _____ .
   a. a cell wall
   b. cytoplasm

4. This drawing represents a _____ .
   a. cross section
   b. three-dimensional view

5. The largest internal feature of this cell is _____ .
   a. a vacuole
   b. a nucleus

6. Inside the nucleus is _____ .
   a. a nuclear membrane
   b. a nucleolus

7. Between adjacent primary cell walls is _____ .
   a. a middle lamella
   b. a chloroplast membrane

8. In addition there is a(n) _____ .
   a. intracellular space
   b. cytoplasmic membrane

H. Look at the drawing below and then respond T if the statements that follow are true or F if they are false.

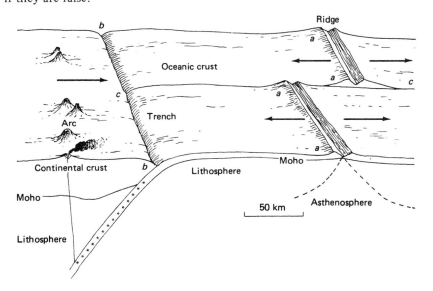

Figure 1-3. Three kinds of plate boundaries: *a-a*, constructive or spreading boundary (oceanic ridge); *b-b*, destructive or collision boundary, marked by a trench and subduction zone; *c-c*, conservative boundary (transform fault). Arrows indicate relative motions of plates. Asterisks mark seismic activity along a Benioff zone. A volcanic arc parallels the trench.

Daniel S. Barker, *Igneous Rocks* (Englewood Cliffs, N.J.: Prentice-Hall, Inc., 1983), p. 3.

_____ 1. This is a representation of a real place on earth.

_____ 2. The illustration shows three types of boundaries.

_____ 3. A ridge is formed in a collision boundary.

_____ 4. A trench results from plates moving away from each other.

_____ 5. Arrows show the direction in which plates are moving relative to each other.

_____ 6. In an a-a boundary the plates spread.

_____ 7. There is no way to appreciate the size of these hypothetical plates, trenches, and ridges.

I. Look at the diagram below and then complete the following paragraph by inserting words from the list.

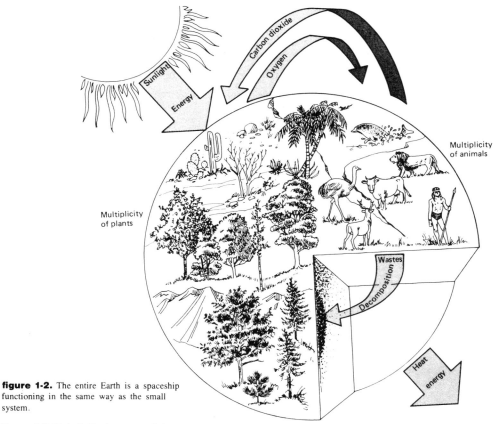

figure 1-2. The entire Earth is a spaceship functioning in the same way as the small system.

Bernard S. Nebel, _Environmental Science: The Way the World Works_ (Englewood Cliffs, N.J.: Prentice-Hall, Inc., 1981), p. 10.

schematic	animals	ecosystem
animals	oxygen	carbon dioxide
energy	decompose	plants
	heat	earth

This drawing is a (1) _____ illustration of the world's (2) _____ . It shows how plants and (3) _____ complement each other on (4) _____. All plants give off (5) _____ and all animals give off (6) _____ . The oxygen is taken in by the (7) _____ while the carbon dioxide is needed by the (8) _____ . Animal wastes (9) _____ and nourish growing plants. The earth receives (10) _____ from sunlight. The decomposition of wastes also produces (11) _____ .

Vocabulary

Alphabetical listing of Vocabulary with reference to the lesson the word comes from

(to) accumulate	5	(to) erect	5
along these lines	1	(to) erode	5
amplitude	3	(to) evacuate	7
apparently	1	eventually	7
as far as we know	1	evident	9
assimilation	5	(to) evoke	9
assumption	5	(to) exude	3
bundle	3	(to) focus	1
cataclysm	7	foreign	9
(to) circumvent	5	(the) former	1
(to) clear up	1	fortuitous	9
(to) clump	9	fracture	7
(to) cluster	9	further	7
conceivably	7	(to) fuse	9
(to) contribute	5	gross	5
cornerstone	9	homologous	9
(to) correlate	7	(to) induce	9
countless	5	infinity	1
conscious	1	intact	3
conspicuous	5	(to) invert	1
(to) deform	7	(the) latter	1
devoid of	5	leakage	3
deliberately	7	(the) literature	9
(to) dissolve	5	(to) manifest	3
(to) distort	1	margin	3
dominant	3	means	7
(to) drain	5	(to) migrate	9
driving force	3	misleading	1
due to	3	negligible	3
(to) elaborate	9	passive	1
emphatically	1	(to) persist	3

plane	7	(to) shrink	1
pore	7	some	5
(to) possess	9	strain	7
precipitation	5	striking	5
(to) presume	5	stringent	5
proliferation	9	subject	1
property	3	tip	3
readily	3	transfer	1
(to) reflect	5	(to) trigger	7
(to) reside	9	unintentionally	7
(to) restrain	7	upside down	1
(to) restrict	5	vapor	5
rim	3	viable	3
said to be	3	(to) wall off	9
(to) scatter	9	(to) withdraw	7
(to) seal	3	worn out	9
(to) secure	3	yet to be determined	3
shock	7		